The Change Doctors
Re-imagining organisational practice

The Change Doctors
Re-imagining organisational practice

Edited by Dr Kathleen King
and John Higgins
with forewords from
Marvin Weisbord and Phil Mix

LIBRI
PUBLISHING

First published in 2014 by Libri Publishing

Copyright © Libri Publishing

ISBN 978 1 909818 06 4

The right of Kathleen King and John Higgins to be identified as the editors of this work has been asserted in accordance with the Copyright, Designs and Patents Act, 1988.

Authors retain the rights to individual chapters

A CIP catalogue record for this book is available from The British Library

Design by Carnegie Publishing

Cover by Helen Taylor

Front cover photograph by Steve Marshall

Printed in the UK by Halstan Printing

Libri Publishing
Brunel House
Volunteer Way
Faringdon
Oxfordshire
SN7 7YR

Tel: +44 (0)845 873 3837

www.libripublishing.co.uk

Acknowledgements

As with any book, this publication would not have seen the light of day without the sustained effort of the authors, the endless patience of their loved ones and the generous support of the publisher. We want to honour and thank all.

However, this book, and all that lead to its inception, creation and publication, has made us particularly aware of the 'unusual suspects', the too-rarely sung heroes who have contributed to the conditions that allow us to learn and to work in the privileged context we call ADOC.

There is, of course, Ashridge. Historically a site of reflection and contemplation, it still has a special quality that rarely fails to leave an impression. We owe a great deal to all those people who, over the ages, built and looked after the house and the truly amazing gardens, and we are indebted to the current staff who make the Ashridge experience as special as it is. And then there is Ashridge Business School. Academic visitors and examiners remind us, rightfully, that we are privileged to be supported in running a programme as counter to current academic trends as ADOC. Whereas many other universities seem to be retreating into a positivist, hyper-rationalist stance, we can experiment, explore, be expansive and play, with the blessing of Middlesex University, our validating body, and Ashridge's management. We treasure these chances.

Finally we want to honour all those great thinkers and practitioners, famous or obscure, popular or ostracised, on whose shoulders we stand. Many come to mind, but we could only name a few, and we dread omitting any. Some have found their way into this book explicitly. Marvin and Philip were kind enough to honour us with their personal contribution. Many are present by implication. It is humbling to realise how much of what we are discovering anew was already well understood at a sophisticated level by previous generations. We can only hope that re-iterating others' wisdom, in a way that is true to our times, might contribute to bringing about the flourishing of our world to which they aspired.

Kathleen King and John Higgins

Contents

Forewords

by Marvin Weisbord and Phil Mix

The purpose of this book, as I discern it, is to help readers discover deeper meaning in their work. The editors showcase first-hand accounts of five graduates of the Ashridge Doctorate in Organisational Change (ADOC) who changed their lives and their work through systematic self-reflection. As students and practitioners of 'Action Research', each invented personal ways of consulting that contradict traditional management practices at every turn. They found that by uncovering hidden dimensions in their own experience they could enable their clients[1] in many fields to achieve new levels of success.

The five women and three men come from diverse backgrounds. They worked in manufacturing and service businesses, the military, academia, and consulting for years before undertaking the learning journey for which this book is a milestone. They have diverse passions – in art, literature, history and the sciences, physical and social. What unites them is a change practice that influences every aspect of their lives, at home and at work, with clients, co-workers, friends, spouses and children. They take on big themes: trust, courage, sensory experience, the oppression of women, the repression of feeling by people at work. They use art, photography, poetry, memoir, myth and analogy – whatever they find bubbling up in them in response to the people they meet and the projects they undertake. They live out the central premise of 'systems thinking': that everything connects to everything else. Their work also suggests something rarely appreciated today, namely that the ancients knew the oneness of mind, body and spirit thousands of years ago.

These twenty-first-century voyagers undertook their life-changing projects in an improbable environment, the Ashridge Business School in Berkhamsted, UK. Some first came to Ashridge seeking masters' degrees as a way of credentialing their work. Some also work at Ashridge as consultants and faculty members. All

---

1   Marvin introduces the term 'clients' here. We continue to use the term throughout the book, after much deliberating on how we could best refer to the people we work with and for. Leaders, managers and consultants alike have people they would 'report to' and people that 'report to them'; they also have peers and clients. Every one of those people is, in one way or another, on the receiving end of the 'gestures' made by the 'change agent'. We did not like the language available to us that speaks of subordinates and superiors, so after some consideration we decided on the term 'clients' in the generic sense of 'the people our efforts are in service of', which seemed the most neutral. We are aware that the term is likely to be more comfortable for consultants, both external and internal, than for leaders and managers. We apologise for not finding a term that more adequately describes what mean.

embrace Action Research as their preferred way of creating workplaces worthy of their clients' aspirations. All undertook the rigours of doctoral research, a multi-year adventure, to feed an insatiable lust for learning.

There is nothing new about Action Research. It was the brainchild of "the practical theorist" Kurt Lewin, a social psychologist and refugee from Nazi Germany, who in the 1920s first proposed a radical form of inquiry – that researchers and their 'subjects' collaborate in studying situations central to their lives and work. Lewin advocated "no research without action, no action without research". He and his students turned this mantra into an experimental practice that led in the decade between 1938 and 1948 to a remarkable series of discoveries: the impact of authoritarian and democratic leadership styles on people's motivation and productivity; the extraordinary capacity of ordinary people for self-management; the way in which participating in important decisions leads people to high commitment and effective action.

I and many colleagues built on Lewin's discoveries to create a successful consulting practice with severe limitations. Because we were grounded in real-time client interactions (rather than expert analysis), the value of our work was harder to discern than in traditional diagnostic reports. Moreover, the rate of change and complexity baffled us as much as our clients. Instead of certainty, we told clients the truth: change means doing something we and they had not done before. You will not find in this book the forms of Action Research that I once practised: team building; survey-data feedback; human relations and leadership skills training; strategic planning; socio-technical work redesign. Many organisations where I used these methods with splendid results no longer exist. Eventually, the same will be true of many of today's brand names.

The five change doctors who reveal themselves here take consulting into places Lewin could not envision. They learn that 'change' does not last long. They learn that hidden creativity exists in every person. They discover that they can change the world by reflecting their life values in every meeting, every day. In reading their stories, we may come to appreciate how to enrich our own lives by a practice simple but not easy – an ongoing inquiry into our world, our workplaces and ourselves.

Marvin Weisbord, October 2013

I was delighted to be asked by Kathleen and John to help introduce *The Change Doctors*. They are two of the most energetically curious, creative and generous scholar–practitioners I know. As well as performing the conventional task of editors, integrating others' contributions into a coherent whole, John and Kathleen fulfil additional, uncommon editing roles as co-inquirers with their colleague contributors.

I was not surprised to find *The Change Doctors* enthralling in content and style: Kathleen and John always are. What did surprise me was how – to a person – the book's contributors were able to combine, in very different yet always-accessible ways, personal disclosure and self-awareness, experience of organisation development work with clients, and sense making of the relationship between the former and the latter.

The work of the *change doctors* and their co-inquiring editors is documented reflexive practice. The *change doctors* and their editors reinforce the immense – and, for clients, sometimes incalculable – value of process consultation that the inquiring and reflexive practitioner brings to organisation development and change efforts.

They validate and encourage organisation development practitioners – like myself – who seek to connect the intrapersonal, including the pursuit of integrity of motivation, with the many complexities of the client systems within which we're asked, and in which we presume, to intervene.

The *change doctors* and their editors encourage us to hold a yin and yang in our practice: challenging ourselves (e.g. How do I feel about starting with where my client is at? Am I willing to risk asking my client to pay for what I would really like to offer them? How important is it to me to quickly prove myself to my client?); while simultaneously accepting our own and our clients' limitations (e.g., in knowledge, skills, integrity of motivation, and risk assessment before intervening).

They invite us as reflexive practitioners to commit to a lifelong journey of personal growth. The *change doctors* and their editors explicitly acknowledge and build upon the work of twentieth-century organisation development pioneers, and they implicitly encourage other practitioners to do the same.

As I read their contributions, I reminded myself of the formative influences on my ongoing development as a reflexive practitioner. They include John Weir (from whom I learned about experiential somatic psychology, owning projections and transference, and archetypal imagery), Ed Schein (from whom I continue to learn about process consultation, the power of culture, and humble inquiry), and Marv Weisbord (from who I continue to learn about working with whole systems, and practitioner presence as intervention). As I work with new forms of organisations, more cross-culturally, and more virtually, I expand my understanding of my learning from my teachers and I integrate that with new theories.

Complex forms of organising, and related system dynamics, are emerging in ways unimagined and unimaginable in the twentieth century, when organisation development was established as a field of practice. In this context, new theories about organising, ways of working, and intervention are emerging – and will continue to emerge – to help practitioners facilitate system task accomplishment and to contain system anxieties. New theories are integrating differences in philosophies and cultural norms (e.g. from the East and West). The *change doctors* and their editors describe organisation development practices – and their theoretical underpinnings – that are more likely to apply across cultural boundaries than are many familiar twentieth-century practices.

For all of these reasons, I believe *The Change Doctors* is a rare and important book for organisation development practitioners. The *change doctors* and their editors have made a significant contribution to the twenty-first-century literature on organisation development.

Phil Mix, November 2013

Introducing the Editors

John Higgins

I have been obsessed with understanding change since I was 15. I have immersed myself in all sorts of perspectives over the years (secretly hankering after a silver bullet I suspect). I've dived into classical economics and the supposed energy of creative destruction. I've been lured by Marxism, its certainty and its politics of conflict. I'm still drawn into the psychoanalytic tradition and am fascinated by the implications of neuroscience and the challenge it presents to the power of the conscious mind.

For a good while now, though, I have been moving away from universal models and grand theories – being drawn instead into an understanding of change as something more ordinary, more wrapped up in the day-to-day of people rubbing along together. This makes sense to me because it grounds my attention in the present and connects change to what is happening in the here and now, rather than in some idealised future or demonised past.

Over time I have also been seeking out a way of studying change that didn't fall into irrelevance – either because its findings were too abstract or because its language was too inaccessible. I have been stumbling into Action Research for a good while now, realising that I am part of any inquiry I make – acknowledging that I am not studying an object called change, but working with people who are engaged in trying to make a difference (and so joining them in that difference-making relationship).

I believe that connecting up theory and practice, self and other, knowing and acting is the key to my making a difference through my habit of writing things down – and my habit of writing is increasingly becoming the method for my own reflexive discipline.

Kathleen King

As a child I was ill-suited to an education that required me to sit still, be quiet and comply. I still find that a challenge. The philosophy and approach that underpin my academic and consulting work can be traced back to those early, difficult experiences. The question "What does it take for people to thrive, and how can I contribute to that?" has never left me. Its particular articulation and focus, and the answers I construct, continue to evolve over time.

Early on in my career I learned that we like to hold on to what is familiar, even if the familiar is painful and wholly unsatisfactory. I discovered some people's extraordinary ability to understand others intuitively and use that talent wisely or otherwise. I learned the importance of a secure environment for human development and learning, and I discovered the significance of the way we exercise power in the delicate matter of human relating. My teachers were children in care.

Their lessons have stayed with me, as I work my way out of a philosophical inheritance of problem-focussed, analytical, human-centric thinking. That process is ongoing. Action Research continues to be a helpful and inspiring discipline. But it is especially the people I meet along the way, fellow (action) researchers, ADOC and AMOC participants, my organisational clients, my colleagues and friends, who continue to provide the safe base from which I can learn to think and act in new ways. This book is a testimony to their influence.

Kathleen King
Kathleen.king@ashridge.org.uk
+447776171473

CHAPTER 1

Introduction

This is a book for people who work in organisations as leaders, consultants, managers or experts[1]. It's for you if you are interested in deepening your understanding of your practice[2], engaging reflexively with the why and how of your work and the assumptions you're working from. It is our aspiration to offer food for thought and provocation to fellow practitioners in the field of organisational change.

In 2012, six graduates of the Ashridge Doctorate in Organisational Change programme (ADOC) came together to continue their collaborative inquiry[3] which had started on the ADOC. As they shared stories of how their doctoral research continued to develop their practice, they decided to make their research and its application available to a broader community of practitioners in an accessible and engaging way. Rather than write for academic or practitioner journals, neither of which reach a wide readership, they decided to write a book that would do justice to the depth of their research, whilst speaking to the day-to-day reality of change practitioners. Their intention was to create a writing process congruent with their doctoral research: an inquiry process in its own right, exploring how their research continues to evolve and influence their current practice. They engaged John Higgins, action researcher and organisational consultant, and me, programme director of ADOC, to be their reflective partners along the way. Our contribution has been to support the writing process by engaging the 'change doctors' – as John called the ADOC graduates – in reflective conversations and offering our notes as a starting point for their further reflection and ultimately for the core chapters of this book. This is editing as Action Research.

Before the change doctors introduce themselves, I will introduce ADOC to you. We believe that the underpinning principles and accompanying practices of the programme are relevant for any (organisational) change effort.

---

1   We use the term 'change agents' on occasions, as shorthand for 'people who support or lead others in the process of organisational change and development'. We are aware that this term is often used to suggest 'people who make change happen'; however, that meaning is not congruent with our view on change.

2   The term 'practice' is used throughout this book. It is a word often used on ADOC, in phrases such as 'reflective practice' and 'professional practice', for example. We use it to indicate a person's work whilst also implying all the thought and skill that are brought to bear on that work, in a way similar to 'craft', or 'métier' in French.

3   We use 'inquiry', rather than the more familiar 'enquiry', in line with the term 'Action Inquiry', which is commonly used in the US as an equivalent to 'Action Research'.

Firstly, how we think about the world and organisations will have an impact on how we engage with them and attempt to enable or initiate change. Therefore, ADOC participants are expected rigorously to examine their view of the world and the foundations of their claims about their practice.

Secondly, Action Research is the methodology of choice on ADOC. Below we explore the different characteristics of Action Research that make it, in our view, particularly valuable for researchers and practitioners alike. We advocate that research is best done with, rather than on people and that belonging to a community of likeminded, supportive and challenging, peers enables learning and change at a profound level (Reason and Bradbury, 2001).

Thirdly, we are interested in 'knowing' that stretches beyond the boundaries of the conceptual and intellectual. With Michael Polanyi (1958) we believe that practitioners know much more than they can readily articulate. ADOC participants are encouraged to engage in arts-based research and representation processes.

Finally, the actual shape of the programme reflects the above principles in different ways. The emphasis on the large group, the extensive work in small Dissertation Supervision Groups (DSGs), the way in which the role of the supervisor is configured and the participant-led-inquiry workshops are all congruent with the above principles. You will also find them present in different ways in the work of each one of the change doctors. I develop them further here, diving in at the deep end with paradigms.

World Views Matter

How we think about the nature of reality, of organisations, change and learning, matters. It influences what we pay attention to, and which actions we expect to lead to particular outcomes. The concepts that govern our everyday functioning show up as metaphors in the language we use to describe our world. Surfacing the assumptions and metaphors that inform our actions and decisions can be surprisingly challenging. Many current organisational practices – including change 'management', our approach to mergers and acquisitions, to performance management and reward structures – result from a mechanistic, behaviourist view of institutions and people. For instance: because it simplifies matters, we like to think of change as measurable on a numerical scale, as if we were measuring a physical distance. We then apply this scale to people's behaviour and (withhold) reward accordingly. Reward systems are often enormously complex and the result of a costly design effort, making it hard even to challenge the assumptions upon which the system is built. Repeated crises in the banking world are just one illustration of our sophisticated reward structures letting us down (Pfeffer and Sutton, 2006).

This mechanistic worldview is deeply ingrained in our culture. Early management theorists sought to establish credibility for their field, transposing language, ideas, principles and analytical thinking practices from natural science, as if people behaved just like controllable variables in a physics experiment. Analytical 'left-brain' thinking assumes cause-and-effect relationships, reduces phenomena down to individual issues, values historical data and seeks certainty and stability. Hence a number of unfortunate assumptions have crept into our managerial language and habits: for example, that there is a world out there that we can know objectively and control; that knowledge can be managed, transferred and generated as if it were a potent gas; that problems can best be solved by finding the single root cause; that managing is a rational endeavour, requiring us to think, engage our mind, without our bodies (since their needs and limitations get in the way) or our emotions (which only cloud our rational judgement and ought to be over-ruled). To quote Marvin Weisbord: "If ever a whole civilization was built on left-brain behaviour, it is the world of work in industrial societies. None of us is immune." (Weisbord, 2012: 258)

'Mechanistic organisations' are highly differentiated, both horizontally and vertically, with hierarchical, centralised control and authority. Roles are tightly defined and closely supervised and there is a proliferation of written rules and procedures, despite the fact that 'doing it by the book' is counterproductive when people are continually confronted with complex and novel circumstances (Pfeffer and Sutton, 2006). Change in organisations seen this way is 'driven', steered from elaborate central plans, which are communicated, mostly top-down, with an emphasis on the repeated telling of so-called key messages. If the desired change doesn't happen according to the plan, we look for faults in the communication strategy, on the assumption that people didn't quite understand what was expected of them and why, or we seek out where the resistance to change might be in the organisation and confront it or root it out.

We are increasingly confronted with the limits of our assumed 'command and control' approach in our family life, our business world and in our wider ecological context. Day and Power (2009) call for an altogether different way of thinking if we want to thrive in our increasingly uncertain, complex and ambiguous world. Organisational leaders and change agents, they argue, will have to think ecologically. Ecological thinking looks for patterns and interdependencies, assumes complex, non-linear relationships, values curiosity, insight and intuition, and works creatively with paradox, uncertainty and contradiction. It requires us to pay attention to the repercussions of organisational strategies on the long-term health of the wider ecosystem. It is grounded in a participatory paradigm, which assumes that our world does not consist of separate entities but of relationships, which we co-create actively and continuously. Moreover, it implies that human beings are connected in an interdependent relationship not only to one another, but also to their other-than-human context. Taking our participation in that relationship seriously requires us to let go of our deeply ingrained assumption that we are masters of the universe. Chief Seattle put it beautifully: "We are not the weavers of the web of life, we are but a strand of it. Whatever we do to the web of life, we do to ourselves".

Cunliffe (2009) similarly ups the ante for change practitioners when she calls for a reflexive rather than reflective practice. The latter, she argues, is grounded in the assumption that we can make logical, objective statements about the world and take a rational, analytical approach to organisational issues. Reflexive practice, on the other hand, challenges those assumptions. Instead, it assumes that we make meaning together, as we go about our organisational business, and that we need to be willing to challenge our most deeply held beliefs and assumptions.

Reflexive practitioners, she says, question their ways of being, acting and relating. She calls this 'self-reflexivity' and considers it the basis for ethical and responsible practice. At an organisational level this involves actively questioning "taken-for-granted strategies, policies and programmes and organisational practices as a basis for understanding how and why these practices might impact people and exclude them from active participation in organisational life" (Cunliffe, 2009: 48). This is no mean feat. The fish, famously, are the last to know about the water. Moreover, in our Western culture we have long admired the Classical rhetorical tradition of oratory and debate. We reward, implicitly if not explicitly, those who can argue their case persuasively and defend their assumptions and opinions vigorously. Action orientation and decisiveness are valued highly in our fast moving world. "Managers hate to sit looking at something from all angles; they like to get on with it" (Weisbord, 2012). Rigorously examining the congruence or lack thereof between our assumptions and our practice slows us down, as does a genuine dialogic orientation, so for much of the time we don't bother to embrace these disciplines in any depth. Moreover, sincerely questioning our long-held assumptions can be scary and can exacerbate the sense of anxiety that change and uncertainty tend to trigger.

In times of high anxiety, the taking of an analytical approach to solving complex and messy problems and relying heavily on external experts who offer blueprint solutions are particularly tempting ways in which to pursue an illusion of control. Psychoanalytic literature calls that instinctive reaction a "defence against anxiety" (Menzies, 1960). Wadsworth (2008) suggests that we will continue to encounter the paradox of people around the world wanting to be maximally self-organising when they are in a healthy, robust state, and conversely wanting to be organised or succumbing to being organised or even coerced when in a vulnerable state. She argues that current conditions of constant and rapid change, widely differing perspectives, conflict and increasing inequality have contributed to the current proliferation of Action Research. Practitioners and social scientists, she believes, are attracted to Action Research and its many variants because of the inherent discipline of staying reflective in action. We agree that creating an organisational context in which reflexive practices and ecological thinking can flourish will require a profound change in the way we approach organisational learning, research, policy making and practice. Social science research that takes place at too great a distance from the action or practice under examination risks getting it wrong or being overly presumptive. Moreover, the research outcomes are often only of genuine interest to the research community, which appears singularly unaffected by the managerial action orientation, and fail to reach the practitioner community. Conversely, practitioners' frenetic planning and acting erodes the time and energy to stop and think about what is done and why, or to inquire more deeply into people's experiences before hurtling onto the next thing (Wadsworth, 2008). In our view, doctoral research needs to make a difference to people's lives. That is why Action Research is our methodological orientation.

Action Research: A Method for Developing Sustainable Organisations?

Effectively, engaging in Action Research reconnects learning and practice with research. Rather than merely bringing researchers and managers closer together – in itself a worthwhile aspiration (Pasmore et al., 2008) – it enables individuals, groups, communities and organisations to develop their own reflexive capacity and become less 'unthinking doers', whilst assisting researchers in embedding their research in the real works of actors and action, in effect becoming more like thoughtful, well-rounded actors (Wadsworth, 2008).

So what does the practice of Action Research entail? Torbert (1991: 220) describes it as "research conducted in everyday life" rather than only within "sanitized experimental environments, survey designs, or reflective, clinical, critical settings". He distinguishes three kinds of inquiry practices:

- First-person inquiry, which is about developing self-awareness and presence of mind and which Fisher and Torbert call "studying oneself in the midst of action" (Fisher and Torbert, 1995). Reason and Bradbury think of it as a person's ability "to foster an inquiring approach to his or her own life, to act with awareness and to choose carefully and assess effects in the outside world while acting" (Reason and Bradbury, 2001). In other words, first-person inquiry practices develop a person's reflexive muscle, in the service of *personal integrity* and effectiveness. Without a first-person aspect, Action Research can lack integrity or fail to surface the blind spots of the individual actors (McGuire, Palus and Torbert 2008).

  First-person inquiry practice is deeply challenging. Torbert (2004) suggests that our intimate relationships, our organisations and social science itself are not familiar or comfortable with close scrutiny. Opening up one's organisational conduct to rigorous inquiry is a not very common practice and tends to be associated with situations of misconduct and trouble. The proliferation of literature following the collapse of corporate giants such as Enron and Lehman Brothers describes vividly the lack of accountability from leaders to themselves, their staff and their stakeholders, and the extent to which corporate behaviour has become immune to scrutiny or challenge.

  We consider first-person inquiry an essential discipline for any organisational practitioner, especially for those embarking on a sustained inquiry into their practice. The emphasis we place on it in ADOC often surprises candidates, especially as many of them have been socialised to research and write in the supposedly neutral and objective third-person voice. The authors in this book comment on the effort and dedication first-person inquiry demands of them, and on the importance of the support from their peers, which brings me to the related subject of second-person inquiry.

- Second-person inquiry can be described as our "ability to inquire face-to-face with others into issues of mutual concern" (Reason and Bradbury, 2001). Unlike many other social-science research practices, second-person inquiry is research *with*, rather than *on*, others. In this process, 'researcher' and participants (not subjects in the traditional sense) remain interested in how power is played out in relationships, with the aim of generating a critical and constructive mutuality. Second-person inquiry seeks to develop the collective abilities of inquiry partners as reflective practitioners. Thus it reduces power differences which get in the way of honest and open communication and generates more complex, nuanced and mutually shared understanding from which to act effectively. This discipline makes it eminently suited as a change methodology and consulting approach. Rather than 'inflicting change' on reluctant subjects or 'driving' the agenda of the powerful players in organisations, it engages people in a collective exploration of the current reality, in the service of informed decision making and joint action.

Second-person inquiry seeks to *foster* mutuality. According to Torbert (2004), inquiring openly in the power play between agents, developing collaborative (dialogic) ways of conversing together, and jointly finding out and agreeing the value of what we are creating together are essential ingredients of mutuality. Fletcher (1999: 114) argues that mutuality is at the heart of relational working: "The essence of mutual vulnerability, mutual openness, and mutual influence is reciprocity – an expectation that the other will be motivated to minimise status differences, to foster growth-in-connection interactions, to respond to and recognise the inevitability of vulnerability and mutual dependence. This mutuality is antithetical to achieving pre-ordained goals. By its very nature, the outcomes of mutual interaction are fluid, unknowable – the essence of creativity rather than management by objectives". Espoused by many organisational development consultants, mutuality is a challenging concept to most managers and researchers. To open one's conduct to profound scrutiny is different from merely submitting one's behaviour to a corporate audit or complying with rules and procedures; and to engage in any encounter expecting or accepting to be changed by it is at the other end of the influencing spectrum from 'driving through' our pre-set outcomes.

- Ethical practice, within a participatory paradigm, requires us to pay attention to the consequences of our actions on the world beyond our immediate space and time horizon. Third-person research does exactly that. It extends questions about power and mutuality in and beyond the human context, exploring power dynamics between people, organisations and their social, cultural and natural environment. Torbert (2004) sees third-person inquiry as being in the service of '*sustainability*': "Without a strong third-person research aspect, inquiry becomes divorced from its extended effects in space and time". It is particularly the long-term impact on society and on our natural habitat that has been deeply and catastrophically neglected in our organisational practices. To pay daily attention to the consequences of our actions – in the short, medium and long term and on our immediate, wider and global context – is a discipline long overdue.

Paying Attention to What Counts as 'Data'

Belenky and colleagues point out that our basic assumptions about the nature of knowledge, truth and evidence profoundly affect the nature of our interaction with the world (Belenky et al., 1997). In search of objectivity, human sciences have carefully attended to excluding tacit knowing, or knowing grounded in intuition, emotions or the body, because it is considered too subjective. "Emotions don't provide reliable data, they interfere with rational decision making", tends to be the going view. Our bodies are similarly unwelcome sources of data, other than 'on top form' and 'full of energy'. In Chapter 7, Sarah Beart will argue that they are only welcome in organisations as a mode of transport for our minds. Abstract, conceptual, intellectual knowledge still reigns supreme in the public arena. Artful, embodied, intuitive knowing is relegated to the private, home sphere and considered irrelevant at best – and inappropriate or suspect at worst (Miller, 1986).

Action Research challenges that privileging of a rationalist bias by drawing on diverse forms of knowing, not just empirical and conceptual but also experiential, presentational and aesthetic, relational and practical (Marshall and Reason, 2008). It honours intuition and tacit knowing, what Shotter (1993) has called "knowing of the third kind". It is the kind of knowing that arises as we engage with others in the process of living. It requires us to look for synchronicity between different ways of knowing across different territories (Reason and Torbert, 2001). It involves extending our knowing "by paying rigorous aesthetic and embodied attention to the ways we receive and respond to the world through our experience, movement, stories, image making, musicality, practice, play and performance... as well as through our ideas and theories" (Heron, 1992).

Seeley (2011) suggests that cultivating greater equity between our different ways of knowing requires systematic attention to what gets noticed and valued; what gets taken seriously and by whom. Quoting Charlton, she argues that it is through *aesthetic* engagement that we can recover our lost sense of our interconnectedness with the rest of life on the planet. She argues that "If we, our organisations and the other-than-human world (upon which we depend) are to flourish then we must carry the responsibility to become more wholly human, ... to actually *live* and *be* in ways which invite the artful *and* the intellectual, the embodied *and* the theoretical, the hearty *and* the heady with equal thoroughness, seriousness and enthusiasm".

William Carlos Williams, in 'Asphodel, That Greeny Flower', says it beautifully:

> It is difficult
> to get the news from poems
> yet men die miserably every day
> for lack
> of what is found there

So What is to be Found in this Book?

At the heart of this book are stories. They are a testimony to the power of Action Research as an approach to research, learning and change. They are accounts by five of the first ADOC graduates of how their sustained process of doctoral inquiry continues to influence their lives and work, and ultimately their sense of who they are and what they are about. Each in his or her own way offers rich food for thought for organisational development practitioners and change agents, be they leaders or consultants.

Here is a little taster of what is in store.

As a highly successful and experienced leader and consultant, establishing trust has been a recurring conundrum for **Jill Hughes** and for her clients. Early in her research process, Jill developed a trust model that was (and still is) hugely appealing to them. But her ADOC learning peers were sceptical and so, deep down, was Jill. Courageously, she pursued her inquiry and took it to a whole new level, asking difficult questions about what it takes genuinely to trust oneself and others. Our current way of organising and doing business is not conducive to proper trust, she discovered. Relationships of mutual collaboration, with respect and integrity, are rare in our corporate world. We are invited to sparkle rather than to glow; to be superhuman rather than to be human with all the fallibility that implies.

Jennifer Carlson's research went full circle, from being outwardly focussed – asking questions about meaningful work – to a relentless inward challenge of deeply held personal assumptions about agency; then back outward into questions of how to hold that agency in the corporate word. Jennifer didn't set out to ask questions about gender but they presented themselves relentlessly in the course of her inquiry. Her growing edge in her practice is to voice the unspeakable, and to challenge the unassailable, in service of a more just, equitable and ethical outcome. However compelling, she is not compulsive. She chooses her causes wisely and her words sufficiently carefully so that she can be heard. The depth of her courage is inspiring.

In our Western corporate world we have banned the body as an embarrassing reminder of our humanity. It is acceptable only as the container of our minds. **Sarah Beart** has traced that development in our history and reinstates our bodies as an invaluable source of knowing. Trusting her embodied experience to be relevant to what is going on for her, for her clients, and in the relationship between them, she offers her insights gently and respectfully. Her practice is one of provocation by stealth: the Trojan mouse that slips into organisations and creates viral disturbance; the acupuncture needle, rather than the surgical knife.

Steve Marshall rediscovered an old love in the process of his research: photography. Armed with his camera and a keen eye for people in their context, he creates an image of his clients, which he offers as an invitation for reflection. Unlike the ubiquitous 360-degree performance review, his process emphasises the *relational* quality of the constructed image and invites dialogue and exploration, rather than defence and isolation.

Knowledge and insight are living social experiences, works in progress. **Kevin Power** is a master at avoiding 'unsafe certainty'. He compares his craft to that of the curator who creates new perspectives on the familiar by attending to previously unexamined connections, unfamiliar juxtapositions and careful attention to context. By refusing to be seduced by premature closure he can be profoundly disturbing, but he does so with care, generosity and empathy, in the process enticing his clients to give of their very best.

About the Shape of this Book

In this introduction I have sought to elucidate the philosophy that informs ADOC, the change doctors and our respective practices. It offers an invitational overview of what is laid out in the pages ahead, much like a catalogue that accompanies an exhibition.

As you read, you will encounter John, my partner-in-editing. As well as supporting the change doctors, John and I engaged in our own inquiry process: an ongoing dialogue deepening our understanding of the change doctors' work, in search of the pattern that connects them with each other and with our own experience of change in organisations and in our lives.

As we revisited earlier drafts of chapters, and earlier conversations, new meaning continued to emerge. To quote John Freeman (2010: xi), "yesterday's certainties serve to fill us with doubt when we view them anew". Freeman relates this experience of "seeing once and then seeing again" with *pentimento*, the way in which draft images surface through the final layer of a painting as the latter becomes transparent with age. We share this 'seeing anew' with the change doctors, who were at pains to point out how much their thinking and practice continue to evolve and how any conclusions can only be a snapshot in time. This discipline of avoiding (premature) closure is an essential part of their practice. Indeed, for Kevin Power it is absolutely at the heart of his consulting work.

In the dialogues that precede each of the change doctors' contributions, we offer some of what we saw in each of their works and in the connection between them, with the intention to invite our readers to 'see for themselves' and to hold our views lightly. True to the dialogic nature of our evolving perspective, we offer our views in a conversational form.

As we work from the assumption that knowledge is personal, as well as social and contextual, we have asked the change doctors to introduce themselves. We have done so too. You can find us on pages xiii–xiv. We turn next to our conversation about Jill Hughes' work, in a conversation that explores the connection between trust, learning and change.

CHAPTER 2

A Dialogue about Anxiety, Safety and Trust

Maybe it was the beauty of the scenery as we walked along the Sussex shore, and the uncomfortable awareness of the stress we humans have put on this delicate ecology; or maybe it was my (Kathleen's) story of the way I had misjudged a change situation at work and caused upset, despite my best intentions; but somehow or other our conversation had strayed into the territory of the anxiety that change brings and the typical psychological defences this can provoke. That's when I mentioned Barry Mason (1993) and his notion of 'Safe Uncertainty'. John was intrigued and asked me to say more about this seemingly paradoxical notion.

Kathleen: Mason suggests that clients tend to seek help when they feel uncertain and unsafe. They come seeking safe certainty. Mason argues that there is no such thing. In his view we can't be certain, not about the present, and especially not about the future. To create an *illusion* of certainty only compromises *safety*. Instead, we need to support people to feel *safe enough* to deal with the uncertainty of the situation, rather than be lulled into a false sense of certainty.

John: Dealing with the actual uncertainty requires us to pay close attention to what is actually happening, rather than what we would like to believe is going on – which is a tough call. It is a prerequisite for making wise decisions about which course of action to take. I have found Heifetz's (1994) distinction between technical and adaptive problems provides a helpful framework when the pull to find 'the easy answer' becomes overwhelming. Our habitual mechanistic 'change management' approaches reinforce our tendency to reduce every challenge to a technical problem, which is an understandable but unhelpful 'defence against anxiety routine' (Menzies, 1960). We know that even the best-laid plans don't survive an encounter with social reality for very long.

Kathleen: Trying to give an 'easy answer', to quote Heifetz, when there is none is of course part of the change agent's very own defensive routine. Facing adaptive challenges requires the leader or change agent to provide a holding environment, the point of which is "not to eliminate stress but to regulate and contain stress so that it doesn't overwhelm" (Heifetz, 1994: 106). This requires, Heifetz argues, a considerable amount of authority – beyond positional power – that is derived primarily from trust. Trust in authority relationships is, in his view, a matter of predictability of values and skill.

John: On the one hand, that makes sense: in order to trust someone I'd want to know that they operate with integrity and that they know what they are doing and are good at it. On the other hand, that seems to me a rather mechanistic view on trust?

Kathleen: Mechanistic, or perhaps instrumental. As Jill discovered in her research, her clients who want help with developing trust in their organisations do start from an instrumental perspective: "If we can get our employees to be sufficiently trusting of us [the senior management, 'the organisation'] they will feel safer and less resistant to the change we have in mind." They want a sure-fire, and preferably fast, way to establish trust so that they can get on with the business. Jill, at one stage in her research, develops a solution – a matrix with recipes, a kind of technical answer – that her clients love, although it's likely to lead to unsafe certainty at best. As she perseveres with her inquiry, and with asking truly challenging questions also of herself, she begins to uncover her own denial process and finds trust of an altogether different level and quality. It doesn't bring certainty but it brings safety, for herself in the first place, as she learns when to trust and when to challenge herself.

John: It reminds me of what a tough call it is to be a good change agent. Consultants are often hired to provide answers and need to resist the temptation to do so, when it is inappropriate or premature. With little positional power they can struggle to make things happen – even simply convening a meeting can be hard work. That in turn can make them more susceptible to being tempted into providing expert answers to validate or justify themselves. Leaders, meanwhile, are impacted by the changes in their organisation and therefore likely to experience the same kinds of fear and anxiety as those around them. Moreover, they will be the subject of projections, whether those are idealising or demonising, and they may become a favourite blame target. Their decisions may cause people to lose their jobs, and they need to be able to cope with that responsibility.

Kathleen: Heifetz calls that *poise* or inner discipline – "the emotional capacity to tolerate uncertainty, frustration and pain". He considers it a prerequisite for creating a safe enough holding environment. On ADOC we believe it is an essential quality of a change agent. It is why self-reflexive practices are the bedrock of ADOC.

CHAPTER 3

The Celtic Queen

By Jill Hughes

My LinkedIn profile introduces me as follows:

> I have worked for over 30 years in leadership development, organisation consulting and change management. Most of my clients are large multinationals such as DSM, ING, Motorola, BP, Ericsson, Arcadis and Aon. In the past two years I have begun working with headteachers in the special needs and secondary sectors, supporting their leadership development. I am also an active trustee of a charity supporting vulnerable children in Northern Namibia.

> My passion is to bring increased vitality to organisations by improving the quality of conversation, trust and relationships. I am particularly interested in designing innovative learning and change interventions with a strong action-learning component. My broad base of experience provides a strong business and results orientation to my work.

This strikes me as having a clear tone and offering an intriguing mix of experience and interests; but it says so little about what is really going on. There is no hint of my concern that the world of work is increasingly hostile to the notion of human flourishing and the doubts I have about the efficacy of my work; it doesn't mention my struggle to trust my creative, intuitive instincts as well as the rational aspects of myself. Yet it was those tensions that created the frustrations, curiosities and possibilities that motivated my doctoral inquiry about trust; and having embarked on that adventure of self-insight and reflection, I have begun to understand myself and the world around me in calmer and kinder ways.

Introduction to the Celtic Queen

My doctoral thesis was entitled: 'An Inquiry into Trust within Consulting Relationships – Confronting My Practice as an Organisational Consultant'. This chapter tells the story of that inquiry, what I discovered about trust (and distrust) and how this has informed and changed my professional life as an organisational consultant working mainly in medium-to-large multinational companies. It also tells the story of how my inquiry became an intense experience of self-development in which I explored and came to understand how I trust myself and how trust shows up in my relationships with others. Joseph Campbell's notion of the "hero's journey" (Campbell, 1949), which claims that all stories have mythical and metaphorical roots, has inspired me and I have borrowed from his work to provide a structure for this chapter. Presenting my experience in this way has given me space for both scholarly and spiritual voices, emotional as well as intellectual insights. It also gives a sense of my lived and re-lived experience of my doctoral journey and something of the wonder of that adventure – an adventure that continues to be an ongoing influence in my life.

The Call to Adventure and the Point of No Return

The call to adventure signifies that destiny has summoned the hero and transferred his spiritual center of gravity from within the pale of this society to a zone unknown.

(Campbell, 1999: 1)

I first discovered Action Research when doing a Master's in Organisational Consulting at Ashridge in 2001–2002. My topic was performance management and some of the unintended consequences that can occur when you categorise people into strata such as the top 10 per cent, middle 70 per cent and bottom 20 per cent of performers. I concluded that much of this effort, done in the service of improving performance, seemed to achieve the opposite effect and was often experienced as arbitrary, constraining and even counterproductive.

It was a sufficiently powerful personal experience to give me the impetus to leave my job as Director of Leadership and Change at Motorola and become an independent consultant. I had started my Master's with a sense of disquiet that all was not well in the world of work, from a human perspective. By the end of my inquiry, I had even deeper feelings of concern. I had worked in Human Resources and Organisational Development roles for twenty years and had been part of a relentless series of redundancies, rightsizings and restructurings in the service of efficiency and productivity improvements. It seemed to me that many organisations had become very lean and very mean places where the notion of human flourishing was given lip service but was not central to the business of commercial life. In becoming an independent consultant, I hoped that being out of the toxic soup for a while would enable me to find fresh motivation, to do work that I felt was going to make a difference in increasing vitality in human relationships within a commercial context.

When Ashridge announced that it was launching its first doctoral programme in organisational consulting (ADOC) in 2005–6, I didn't hesitate in signing up, though I was aware of the potential challenges. I knew it would require a serious commitment in terms of time and I was already busy with my work as an independent consultant; my two children were now demanding teenagers; the fees required a considerable investment; and as my husband had recently become self-employed, our income was not particularly secure. Finally, I expected it to be an intensely personal, perhaps even painful and disorientating, experience. However, I didn't dwell on these difficulties for long. The lure of ADOC and the desire to learn and reflect on how the world of work could be a better place were far stronger than any concerns.

My first difficulty was in deciding my research topic. I had assumed that most doctoral inquiries require you to have an atavistic itch that demands to be scratched and I didn't have that. However trust/distrust seemed to be a subject that had been in my subconscious cupboard for a while. In the late nineties, I had been part of a team in Motorola which had spent two years researching, developing and facilitating dialogue workshops, with the intention of enabling deeper levels of openness and connection between employees and their managers through better conversations. However, a round of redundancies had seemed to obliterate the impact of this work, with record low levels of trust being recorded in the annual employee survey. I remembered a conversation with one of my team colleagues at the time in which we'd talked about whether trust was actually possible, or even desirable, in the world of commercial companies. This had haunted me ever since.

The impact of 9/11 and the high-profile failures of organisations such as Enron at the end of 2001 meant that trust was big news, and the evidence of a serious systemic decline in trust was widely documented. Reynolds (1997: 5) contends that "only 15% of the British public trust multinational business to be fair and honest". Bruhn (2001) describes the many polls in the US that chart a decline in trust in organisations, politics and in society in general. Yet trust seemed to be the Holy Grail for many of my clients and much of my work was predicated on their desire to create more trusting cultures. My curiosity was caught by a central conundrum: if trust was such a good thing (for people and for profit) and everybody wanted it, why was it so difficult to create? Why did distrust seem to be on the rise?

I found myself at the first engagement workshop of ADOC in June 2006, sitting in a circle with twelve other fellow students and three members of faculty. There was a frisson of anticipation, anxiety and excitement in the room. I had written an initial paper outlining my interest in the topic of trust and was hoping it would be enough to give me a start, though I had no idea whether it would be enough to sustain me throughout four years. I looked around the circle and wondered who would stay the course and who would drop out. As I was thinking this, one clear certainty popped into my head. I wrote in my journal, "Whatever happens, I will be one of the ones still here at the end." I had called on my stubborn, competitive and determined instincts and I knew from experience that once I had summoned those parts of me, I was at the point of no return.

Entering a New and Strange Land

This fateful region of both treasure and danger may be variously represented; as a distant land, a forest, a kingdom underground, beneath the waves or above the sky, a secret island, lofty mountaintop or profound dream state.

(Campbell, 1999: 1)

I realised what a new and strange land I had entered when I acknowledged the power and central importance of first-person inquiry. When my gaze turned inwards and I asked myself questions such as "What is going on here? Why am I feeling what I am feeling? What are my patterns of sense making?", my ordinary life became extraordinary. My "kingdom underground" was the discovery and exploration of my own sense making and inner complexity.

Here is an example of a journal entry that was written in the minutes before a telephone call from a client in which I was expecting to be fired:

> A flutter of nerves is playing around my lower rib cage. As my attention focuses on my body, the heat turns up and a shot of hot anxiety begins melting my insides. I am waiting for a call from my biggest client. I have been told by a colleague that he is unhappy about my behaviour at a recent training event in which he believes I allowed a group of middle managers to openly criticise a new corporate initiative. He is concerned he cannot trust me to support the organisation's efforts appropriately. The intellectual part of me is skilled in reframing this sort of situation… seeing it as an intriguing example of the tensions around the consultant–client relationship. Yet at this precise moment, all my intellectual knowing has not ameliorated my feeling of dread as I wait for the phone to ring. There is a part of me ready to explain myself but my overwhelming feeling is one of deep foreboding. I feel small, dented and insecure.

(Hughes, Personal Journal[1], 2006)

Although a small snapshot of the minutiae of my thoughts and feelings, there seemed to be a tantalising possibility that this might contain clues to deepen my understanding of my topic. There is an intriguing mix of the confident voice that can reframe this potential rupture of trust as a typical tension between client and consultant, combined with a very different quality of emotional turmoil, vulnerability and anxiety. My early hunch was that the existence of such paradoxical energies might well be significant in understanding more about the phenomenon of trust.

My first instinct hadn't been to go down this path. Initially, I took a more conventional approach by reading what other people had written about trust. I began in a haphazard way reading from multiple perspectives – sociological, psychological, philosophical, political, anthropological and economic. Eventually I whittled this down to four domains of interest: the feminist perspective on trust; psychotherapy and trust; moral philosophy and trust; and critical social science and trust. But it was still a daunting spread of ideas and concepts. I found myself becoming increasingly dispirited about what I was actually learning and discovering. Here is an extract from my journal that captures my sense of impotence:

> I feel overwhelmed by the enormity of my topic, stunned into torpor by the difficulty and complexity of it. I view my inquiry as a tiny little thing of insignificance, half-hearted in its rigour and spent in its sense of direction. I have been working and thinking about it for nearly two years, and I sit here with a sense of having little to show, little to say.

(Hughes, Personal Journal, May 2008)

When I shifted my curiosity in trust as a phenomenon 'out there' to an inquiry about trust 'within me', my inquiry took on a new vitality and life, as well as strangeness and a sense of danger. I was beginning to agree with those who claim that, despite the aspiration of traditional science to inquire into the nature

---

1   An important part of our first-person inquiry practices is keeping a reflective journal for the duration of the Doctorate.

of things, through experiments and gathering data, it is inherently unsatisfactory: "The status and significance can only be explored from within, by full engagement in the human condition." (Heron, 1996: 1)

Yet this shift from the objective to the subjective also created its own tension. I suspect this might be common for action researchers who have moved away from positivist research principles. I worried about solipsism and excessive self-interest; I questioned if subjectivity could ever be regarded as valid and whether my reflections could be regarded as reliable or even truthful; I wondered if I was playing into the hands of those sceptics who might regard such personal disclosure as self-indulgent and irrelevant, for the purposes of furthering our knowledge about my topic of trust.

Yet once I had acknowledged that there is a fundamental elusiveness to anyone's ability to describe and understand their inner world, I became less concerned about notions such as accuracy, truth and reliability, which seemed to apply objective principles to subjective experience. Richardson and St. Pierre (2008: 478) summarise this well when they say "there is no such thing as getting it right, only getting it differently contoured and nuanced".

My dissertation supervision group (DSG) and tutor also encouraged me to explore deeper levels of subjective inquiry. They told me they found some of my earlier writing (such as the academic analysis of other people's ideas on trust) "boring", "dense" and "speeded up to the point of disinterest". I am not sure why this came as a surprise to me because I often experienced conventional academic writing as dry and lacking vitality. Olesen (2000: 394) observed that "researchers seem to have lost the human, passionate elements of their research" and goes on to say that the "individual is not inserted into the study but is the backbone of the study". So although feeling self-conscious about my angst-ridden ramblings, I was fortified by my intention to be rigorous, disciplined and heartfelt. Torbert (2001) encourages the researcher to "be concerned for the quality of our moment-to-moment experience of our awareness"; Rogers (2004: 128) describes this as "self-conscious awareness" where people are free "to live subjectively as well as be aware of it". I found the experience of standing outside myself and responding to different interpretations of what might be going on for me to be a powerful personal development experience and my initial reservations dissipated as I was drawn in.

Different Ways of Knowing, When in Strange Lands

Participatory Action Research encourages extended epistemologies and by that I mean other ways of knowing in addition to the intellectual or rational. For me writing poetry became very important. Reason (1997: 3) would describe this as presentational knowing, where I could access my "felt attunement with the world and the primary meaning it holds for me". Fontana and Frey (2008: 149) claim that poetry can be a powerful way to "encapsulate a welter of feelings and emotions, a life story, a tragedy, a moment of sorrow or of utter joy". Brady (2008: 529) says the "ultimate aim of poetic expression is to touch universal meaning through the particular".

I found these ideas particularly powerful because they seemed to give me permission to experiment with ways of knowing that I had previously not accessed. I had never written a poem before my doctoral studies, yet by the end I chose to include eight of them in my final thesis. This in itself represents quite a shift in my ontological and epistemological perspective of the world – from a bias toward prose and intellectual knowing to that of honouring and valuing subjectivity and creativity.

Writing poetry became a way for me to access my inner world. It seemed to allow me to write what needed to be written (without smoothing out the edges and over-rationalising) with a sense of freedom and creativity. At the same time, it felt disciplined and exquisitely distilled – a turbo-charged summary with expansive and multiple interpretations. Here is how I explained my process in my thesis:

> I start off with a phrase, word or a memory that has been haunting me for a while. At this point in the process, I have some ideas of direction and meaning that I want to write about but shortly after starting to write the poem, a slipstream of energy takes over and words flow from the keyboard. In allowing this, I frequently find myself in unexpected territory not intended at the start.

(Hughes, 2010: 18)

Finding myself in unexpected territory a lot of the time was a strange experience – both enjoyable and also embarrassing. I felt self-conscious about it and had consciously to stop my analytical and intellectual instincts from becoming too present. I often wrote a poem as an afterthought that I hoped might add something to a piece of writing. However, the experience of writing a poem seemed to change something and I would become aware of how much richer both the writing and the poetry were. Bringing both together I could say "Yes, this is me!"

Here is a poem I wrote after an extremely difficult meeting that left me very upset.

A Difficult Conversation

The difficult conversation
Cracks my resilient veneer
Helpless fragments like soft stars melt in
Into boundless waters

I see a ladder, it's always been there
I step on to a rung and down into
The murky calm, quiet and accepting
The surface commotion receding

And there within the silt of doubt
Buried but not hidden
Is the small bright treasure
Of my loving heart

(Hughes, 2010)

There is something about the simplicity of this poem that feels personal and intimate. I am surprised how touching I find expressing how "my loving heart" has been dimmed by "doubt" and "silt". The ladder is a metaphor for introspection and reflection that has a very different quality to the "commotion" and noise going on above – "calm, quiet and accepting". How different this feels from the earlier journal entry in describing the ways I deal with criticism. In the example of waiting for the client call, I am full of a feeling of worthlessness. Here my veneer of resilience has a brittle quality and when it shatters, there is a sense of beauty and softness as the fragments are absorbed into a sense of myself that is boundless. In this way poetry released a quality of acceptance, warmth and calmness about how I am coming to understand and experience the phenomenon of trusting myself. It is an experience of healing in that I am allowing this quality of care towards myself to be released.

A Road of Trials

Once having traversed the threshold, the hero moves in a dream landscape of curiously fluid ambiguous forms where he must survive a succession of trials.

(Campbell, 1999: 19)

So although at times I found the experience of immersing myself in my own sense making to be joyful and touching, it could also be dangerous, dark, tricky and disturbing territory – so much so that I could describe my doctoral inquiry as one long succession of trials. There were plenty of unimaginable torments that I journalled and reflected upon. Here I have created an illustrative narrative of my "road of trials" during 2007–2008 that offers some insights into my topic of trust and the invaluable role of my DSG.

About six months after I started ADOC, I broke my hip as a result of a misdiagnosed stress fracture after running a marathon. At the time I viewed this as a bit of bad luck – a serious but straightforward sporting injury. Within my inquiry I was wrestling with what it meant to trust myself, but in dealing with my broken hip I was choosing to suppress and distrust what my body was telling me. Here is a journal entry written at the time that suggests that although I had some awareness of this pattern, I was unable or unwilling to change it.

16 April 2007

My broken hip has morphed into a dinner-party story and not a personal tragedy. The tests are clear and I tell myself I'm dealing with a straightforward recovery from an operation. I notice that I am willing myself to get over this as soon as possible. My friend Gordon took me aside at a party and encouraged me to "make more out of it." Take a few weeks off work. Allow other people to run after me. I think about my work schedule for the next few weeks. It's packed. Lots of travelling (including a trip to Bangkok) and hardly a day free. At the January workshop Bill said I am "unstoppable, a bit otherworldly". At the time it didn't really resonate, but perhaps he has a point. What is so interesting is that it hasn't even occurred to me to "take things easy" or to "make more out of this". I decide to make a conscious effort to be kinder to myself. I will let go of giving myself a recovery goal and try to love my crutch more.

I went into the city for a coaching meeting today. It was the first time I have braved the rigours of the tube since the op. Being kind to myself, I booked a cab for the mile-long journey from house to station. With such a luxury, I felt I could afford to put on some nice shoes with heels.

With 96 minutes each way, four tube changes and miles of stairs and corridors, it turned out to be a teeth-gritting struggle. The "chump chump" of the rubberised tip of the crutch on each interminable steel-tipped step. Up and down, down and up, one dogged step at a time. The pain in my hip and knee consuming everything and dragging my progress. At one point I got to 8 out of 10 in my pain scale and felt on the verge of panic. The crush of people around me all going twice as fast, the dimmed and dreary underground lighting making this an archetypal scene from hell.

I needed to relax, stay calm and get back to 6–7 in the pain range. I fixed my eyes to the floor and planted the crutch tip safely on the slippery tiled floor, slowing my breathing and only thinking about one step at a time. The escalators (blessedly welcome) were not as friendly as I'd hoped: they were going too fast for me to manage easily with my crutch arm. And all the time those silly shoes pitched me forward at an agonising angle. I am down to 7 in the pain scale and congratulate myself for each bit of progress. What a girl! What a trouper! What an idiot!

(Hughes, Personal Journal, 2006)

I may say I am an idiot but it is the notion of being a trouper that resonates. I was framing gentleness as weakness and listening to my body as indulgent. My DSG were frank in their feedback to me. They were not impressed with my physical bravery, which they regarded as misplaced and a symptom of denial and suppression. I was stunned and tearful in the face of what I experienced as their harsh treatment of me and at first I felt cut adrift from them. It took some time for me to realise they had my best interests at heart and, although painful, to acknowledge my own blind spots and destructive patterns. Their feedback and support became an essential part of my development process. Many doctorates are somewhat lonely affairs with only you, your topic and your tutor. The ADOC structure that included peers who were both supportive and appropriately critical was an important part of my learning experience.

The years 2007 and 2008 were exceptionally busy for me in terms of volume of work. It could be said that I was at the height of my powers – much in demand and valued by my clients. I came to know myself through the persona of the anxious overachiever, constructing trust as being formed on the basis of me being able to perform beyond other people's expectations.

I am rewarded with repeat business if my evaluations are high, and dropped if they are low. In my journals and in my practice I refer to the "tyranny of my own success" and also the enormous impact of failure (a sense of depression and worthlessness) through the eyes of others.

(Hughes, Personal Journal, 2007)

This is a fairly ruthless view of my client relationships, where I have constructed trust as fragile and one sided, leaving me with a sense of powerless and anxiety. This resulted in an increasing disconnection between my inner world and this outer world of achievement.

> A horrible night. Wine, sleeping pills still prevented me from sleeping till after 5am. I feel terrible – headache, red eyes, tired, depressed, longing for this thing to be over. And yet even in this difficult place I am still interested in the participant experience. Are they connected? Interested? It speaks to me about some core values I have around hard work, professionalism, care and also to the shadow side of this – anxiety and its exhaustion and an overbearing sense of responsibility.

My DSG had encouraged me to notice my patterns of sense making and the nature of my dynamism within the context of my work, but I was only just beginning to understand its complexity. At the same time I was also beginning to understand the pervasiveness of distrust in the organisations I work in; how this triggered the persona of myself as an 'anxious overachiever' where I privileged my masculine qualities of resilience and determination to the detriment of my feminine qualities – such as my intuition and concern with physical well-being and harmony. In navigating this road of trials there was excitement and affirmation (financial gain, professional accolades and so on) as well as a cost – insomnia, chronic anxiety and worry about meeting other people's expectations. I was realising that I seemed to be living in a world that seemed more based in distrust and fear than trust and love.

Meeting with the Celtic Queen

> As he progresses in the slow initiation which is life, the form of the goddess undergoes for him a series of transfigurations. She can never be greater than himself, though she can always promise more than he is yet capable of understanding.

(Campbell, 1999: 81)

As my inquiry progressed and I was being confronted by my own complexity, I was struggling to find a way of making sense of myself. My curiosity was caught by the Jungian notion of archetypes as a way of capturing an essence of multiple ego orientation and breadth of sub personalities. The Jungian idea of archetypes as being "a self-portrait of the instinct" (Jung, 1957) seemed to be an interesting and imaginative idea (the poet within me thinking "this is great – an adventure into my psychic cosmos!"). At the same time, I was sceptical, as it sounded a bit fanciful. So I was attracted to the notion and at the same time holding some caution about it. That caution was initially embedded in some practical questions around how an archetypal view of myself could be useful. Wilber (1996) argues that archetypes can be useful in describing both current and future potentials.

> Archetypal gods and goddesses… are simply a collection of typical and everyday self-images and self-roles available to men and women… that represent typical potentials. And those mythic roles are very useful… to bring forth that potential in your own life.

(Wilber, 1996: 195)

I found the literature dominated by masculine archetypes such as warriors, heroes and jesters – some of whose qualities I recognised in myself – but found relatively few feminine archetypes that might inspire my thinking. For example, the Crone Goddess is a well-known archetype representing older women's wisdom and insight, but has a lot of negative cultural associations – ugly witches, something to be feared and so on. It seems to reinforce the feminist view that the patriarchal society has discouraged girls from accepting their own wisdom, and that the majority of women are intimidated by their power as well as their own physical deterioration.

This was interesting and thought-provoking but ultimately not particularly helpful to me. I realised that finding my archetype was not going to happen by reading other people's writing and taking one "off the shelf" in the hope that it would fit. My process was going to have to be more personalised and less politicised by feminist rhetoric. We had talked a lot about archetypes in the DSG and Sarah suggested that Maeve, one of the Celtic Queens, might be an interesting character for me to explore. As a Scot this had some appeal and the notion of Celtic Queen "clicked" (a very resonant and descriptive term from Jung (1983: 185)), not as another label or identity that I was taking on, but rather as a more mysterious, instinctual and universal way of knowing myself.

As I thought about the Celtic Queen working in an environment where the client is constructed as Client King, it created a potent image of commercial royalty! Here is an extract from my year-three paper as an example of how I was becoming sensitive to the quality of that potent mix:

> It provokes an idea that I, as a 'Celtic Queen' consultant, bring in something of an equality of status with the 'Client as King', with a scintilla of the feminine and all that might suggest (both the sexual, devious, underhand and the empathetic, warm and relationally skilled qualities of the feminine). After a recent meeting with a CEO in which I was discussing helping him with his senior team, he commented after the meeting on how he had experienced our meeting:

> I am seduced by your ideas, approach. I have felt appropriately challenged. I thank you for that. It doesn't happen often. I am committed to doing this and want my people to experience what you have done with me today.

> (Hughes, Personal Journal, 2009)

Phrases like "seduced by your ideas" and "appropriately challenged" seem to give meaning to the Celtic Queen who has both masculine and feminine qualities. The trust that the Celtic Queen evokes in this example is due to her being skilful, capable and perhaps a bit bolshie – while at the same time being charming, empathetic and perhaps a bit devious.

As this archetype became more figural for me, I found aspects of her in much of my work. I noticed that frequently I responded with both a competitive and charming energy towards clients, who were often quite hostile about investing time in relational development. Here is a poem that tells a story of when I worked with a group of senior managers who described themselves as "natural born killers". The Celtic Queen in me, undeterred by their intimidating version of themselves, designed an experiential activity with boxing gloves intended to illustrate the difference between dialogue and discussion. However, they became so enthusiastic about hitting each other that I had to stop the activity before someone got hurt.

The Maximum Score

The boxing gloves flail softly
Swiping and cuffing
Red orbs flung from red faces
Tightly defended and closed
In for the maximum score

No use for dialogue
No space for elegant defeat
Energy pouring outward
Making a lot of noise
To get the maximum score

Laughter and smiles all round
What a great idea
To teach us hitting skills
Please come back again
You've got the maximum score

(Hughes, Thesis, 2010)

The poem released a sense of knowing in me that went much deeper than an intellectual awareness. I describe the instinctive reaction of the participants to hit each other ("swiping and cuffing") and how this aggressive outflow of energy renders the ideas of dialogue and defeat as weak and useless. The notion of competition is suggested in the participants' preoccupation with getting the maximum score even though the activity was set up to contradict such a concept. This is also a metaphor for my own Celtic Queen energy that also wants to make an impact. The 15 participants all gave me the maximum score in their assessment after the workshop, but implicit in the idea of "a maximum score" is a sense of pointlessness causing me to question whether I am doing the right work, in the right place, with the right people.

When I looked to transcripts of conversations with colleagues, stories of siege, embattlement and stress are everywhere. Here is an extract from a story told by Martha, a colleague in the USA, talking about how she responded to a brutal culture of work:

So on top of the politics already there, you had this racial tension. And we had a mayor who used to walk through the halls saying "I hate white woman, I hate white woman!" So you are working in a relatively hostile environment. The next day I went into Peggy, my boss's office and I said, "I've got it, we are the spear chuckers in their play!" And we started to elaborate on it and we were imagining them in the breastplates and the helmets and long hair. And we were in the back and doing this thing and I can't tell you why it was so funny, but we were howling.

And when she left, I gave her one of these helmets and the braids. She is black, by the way. It was very funny. So there is a certain bonding, that having gone through these experiences, you just form these incredibly deep relationships and now those are the people I'm going to talk about, um I would like to work with. And you know they trust me, we have been through the war together.

(Hughes, Thesis, 2010)

My Celtic Queen archetype was in danger of becoming a Warrior Celtic Queen, where the only way trust could be forged was with fellow soldiers surviving against the odds in the battlefield of organisational life. It was as if the only thing I could be certain about was that distrust is endemic in organisational settings. It felt that my inquiry into trust was at a nihilistic dead end.

The Runes of Wisdom

Requires that the hero begin the labor of bringing the runes of wisdom… back into the kingdom of humanity.

(Campbell, 1999: 113)

I suspect it is normal to feel lost and depressed at times when doing a doctorate, but this was particularly inconvenient timing. I had been invited to present my findings to a client group of senior managers, who had a great interest in developing more trusting relationships with their customers. I felt nervous and inadequate about owning up to my abject state of confusion. In the early hours of a sleepless night before the workshop, I sketched out a ubiquitous two-by-two model as an attempt to offer a summary of my work so far.

The speed at which I did this suggests it had been sitting somewhere in my subconscious for a while. I had been greatly preoccupied with the idea that there might be a difference between feminine and masculine versions of trust. This probably had its roots in the work of the moral philosopher Annette Baier, whom I greatly admired. She describes the feminine construct of trust as centring around emotions, feelings and love; and the masculine around reason and obligation. Her contention (Baier, 1994: 10–11) is that "trust nicely mediates between reason and feeling"; her encouragement to develop a moral theory "which looked at the conditions of proper trust" was a big "Aha" moment for me.

In my model, I took out the explicit references to masculine and feminine (thinking that they might be too provocative) and re-titled them "transactional competence" and "relational connection", with an alliterative trio of titles – pragmatic, personal and proper trust. I gave bullet-point descriptions for each to produce the following framework:

A framework to deepen our understanding

	Low — Relational connection — High	
High	**Pragmatic trust** - Expertise, known track record - Agreement of rules and mutuality via explicit contracts - Reliability and consistency in delivering agreed outputs - Transactional and rational	**Proper trust** - Synthesis of pragmatic and personal trust - A dynamic dance dependent on context - Not easily sustained
Low	**Distrust** - Human relationships characterised by a going process of minor rupture and repair - Intensity of relationship prior to major distrust episode will influence the likelihood of repair	**Personal trust** - Psychological safety - sharing of vulnerability and 'true' feelings - Unconditional positive regard of the other - absolute trust - Relational and emotional

(Vertical axis: Transactional competence — Low to High)

(Horizontal axis: Relational connection — Low to High)

I immediately worried that this marked a regression back to positivist principles, as I had come to regard the notion of models generally as unsatisfying attempts to codify complexity. Trust models proliferate in the business literature as writers attempt to describe the nature of the phenomenon. Maister, Green and Galford (2002) describe trust by way of a formulaic equation (with four elements of reliability, credibility, intimacy and self-interest) and describe a five-step process to achieve it: engage, listen, frame, envision and commit. Covey (2006) favours a three-part categorisation of trust which he describes as blind trust, smart trust and distrust, and identifies 13 behaviours that will contribute to creating smart trust; suggesting there is a "sweet spot of mutual trust" and draws a graph to explain it.

I choose these examples as they represent well-intended attempts to understand a complex phenomenon and to offer practical advice. However, in my inquiry I had dismissed them as limited and, if they had any usefulness, it was as a starting point to stimulate collaborative sense making and dialogue, supporting a move to a deeper level of understanding.

So what was going on: why had I chosen to do the very thing I'd been critical of others for doing? I suspect I was privileging a form of pragmatic trust that was concerned with presenting myself as someone with professional competence and knowledge. In doing so, I was projecting my assumption that this would establish a trustful connection. At one level this was affirmed – the managers gave a positive response to my matrix, there was a good quality of discussion and an invitation to return to run other workshops. I remember feeling relieved and pleased by their reaction. At another level, however, I was left with a lingering and troubling sense of disappointment.

By not sharing my inner uncertainty, that personal and proper forms of trust might not even be possible in a commercial environment, I had in some way misled them about the true state of my inquiry. In offering them a tidy explanation of the phenomenon of trust, I had implicitly suggested that, although personal and proper trust are challenging (depicted by a squiggly line), they are possible.

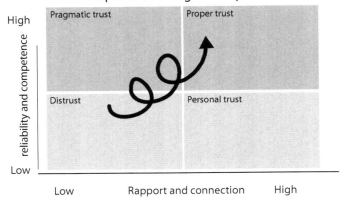

Proper trust – a dynamic non linear process – capable of being developed

In the days after the workshop it increasingly felt like a missed opportunity. I could have experimented with some alternative ways of exploring the topic – poetry, archetypal images, streams of consciousness, for example – rather than assume they would be disappointed if I hadn't showcased 'expertise'. As seasoned (and possibly sceptical) managers, they might also have been ambivalent about models and been even more appreciative of a more provocative approach. Perhaps if I shared more of my inner vulnerability and confusion, this might have encouraged a mutual sharing of our 'real selves' that would have created an even deeper connection of personal trust.

After this meeting, I encouraged myself *to hold loosely to the notion of frameworks*! Yet I continued to have an ambivalent relationship with my model throughout my inquiry and it refused to go away completely. I even experimented using it as a diagnostic to assess clients' bias of their trust preference when pitching for new business. If a client seemed concerned primarily about my track record and experience, I would offer them the best pragmatic version of myself and at the same time attempt to pull us gently towards more personal contact. Equally, if I found myself with someone who seemed to work on a more intuitive or intimate level, I would respond with a similar quality of relational energy and at the appropriate time also offer them evidence of expertise and professional competence. I carefully documented my skilful dance between pragmatic and personal forms of trust and evidenced the efficacy of this by winning a lot of new business. However, rather than concluding I had discovered the elixir of trust, it slowly dawned on me that I had become a skilful salesman with a lot of contracts but not much "proper trust", as few of these new client relationships deepened or developed beyond transactional levels of trust.

I eventually forgave myself for creating the model. I acknowledged that it had been useful in describing the complexity of trust and it had been a resonant way to describe my direction of travel, away from the masculine/pragmatic forms of trust (which I was increasingly viewing as a version of distrust) towards an increasing attraction to the domain of personal trust. This is a domain characterised by shared vulnerability, mutual intimacy and psychological safety.

Here is a poem that describes the beginnings of this shift of my centre of gravity:

My Winged Chariot

My winged chariot slows and stumbles
Towards the shimmer of an autumnal horizon

My shiny grip loosening and lessening
And in its place a stranger sense of self

Its melancholy layers and creative glow
Alerting me to its dangerous welcome

The grieving child stands sadly, full of longing
Her destiny folding into mine

(Hughes, 2008)

The "shiny grip" and "creative glow" became powerful metaphors to describe different qualities of my consultant energy. "Shiny" relates to the moments in which, as consultants, we take centre stage, deliver a performance, show our expertise beyond any doubt and satisfy our audience that they have contracted the 'right' person. The metaphor is one that evokes a brightness and warmth that attracts people to it. It is dramatic, entertaining and compelling. Simultaneously, "shiny" also suggests light that is deflected from a hard surface back to others; that distances people from it as you cannot look it in the eye or connect with it on equal terms. My personae of anxious overachiever, my expertise with pragmatic forms of trust and my archetype as Celtic Queen seemed to belong within this spectrum of light. This might seem impressive but it always casts a shadow and the brighter the shine, the darker the shadow.

"Glowing" refers to those moments in my consulting experience when we find ourselves in relationships with others where we can truly be ourselves. Where we think collaboratively with colleagues and clients, with mutual integrity and respect. The metaphor suggests an inner energy that is softer, that radiates outwards with warmth, appreciation and acceptance. "Glowing" acknowledges we are all human beings – both competent and fallible – and in this world of great uncertainly, needing to know the answers is not always the most important thing. Simultaneously, "glowing" can also be seen as fuzzy, vague and unnoticed. Some may say it is less relevant in the world of work, where clarity, certainty and action are valued. In this respect it felt both strange and dangerous to me, but my attraction to its qualities was clear and I would say almost inevitable.

My rune of wisdom was to conclude that, if trust were to be found and sustained, it would be within the domain of personal trust and within the spectrum of the energy of glow. Yet was this possible in a context of my work, where the commercial aspects of consultant–client relationships seem to dominate? The preoccupation with deliverables, metrics and value for money seemed to create an irreconcilable tension between return on investment and the inherent ambiguity of relational work. The dominant feature of how work was contracted, and awarded, in my client contexts increasingly seemed to privilege a narrow definition of work within the construct of 'the project' or 'the intervention'. In particular, informal relational work, that was often just as important, was seldom recognised or recompensed. It seemed the notion of partnership was familiar rhetoric, but there was a reluctance to articulate and pay for it. Moreover, there was sometimes suspicion towards consultants who forged deep relational connections with senior managers. Images of slippery consultants with silver tongues, lurking in the shadows of senior managers who were caught in the thrall of a dangerous, dependent and expensive advice taking relationships came to mind.

This left me with some disarming questions. Were the levels of distrust I experienced in my organisational work inherently hostile to the integrity of relational practice that I aspired to? Was the inner work I had done to trust myself unlikely to be sustained and nourished in such a toxic outer world? Was the quality of partnership in consultant–client relationships actually possible in an environment that seemed to be increasingly moving toward commoditising consulting relationships? Where in the context of my practice could 'personal trust' be nurtured and sustained?

The Magic Flight Home

The hero is then explicitly commissioned to return to the world with some elixir for the restoration of society...

(Campbell, 1999: 141)

When I wrote up my main findings in my thesis in 2010–2011 it was to conclude that distrust was pervasive and 'personal' forms of trust were rare in the world of work. I went on to state that relational work was often undervalued and the commoditisation of consultant–client relationships made the notion of partnership difficult. Although it could be argued that these conclusions were neither radical nor new, I contended that my contribution to the world of knowledge was in explicitly calling this to our attention. In describing the pervasiveness of distrust and the challenges to partnership within consultant–client relationships, I hoped to reveal what Chase (2008: 80) would describe as the "stranglehold of oppressive meta-narratives" and, by naming this "oppressive meta-narrative", open up a dialogue which could have significance and impact beyond the scope of my inquiry. I hoped that my heartfelt and rigorous autoethnographic inquiry would be regarded as a credible account of my lived experience.

At the start of my inquiry I intended to come to, if not "some elixir for the restoration of society", at least a few insightful conclusions about how trust might be achieved in the contexts I work in. So ending in this place might once have felt like a disappointment. However, that seemed to belong to the shiny world of the Celtic Queen, with an outward show of confidence and certainty – whereas ending where I did felt more real; more ambiguous. It was as though one inquiry was ending and another was beginning and it brought me to a point of decision. If my aspiration was to develop deeper relational integrity characteristic of 'personal' trust, then something had to change. My inquiry had confronted my practice as an organisational consultant and my way of being as Celtic Queen in that world. Here is my last poem, written as I completed my final thesis, where I describe my decision to take a six-month sabbatical to reflect on my future.

In My Own Time

My shield, tucked underarm
Weapons and wiles asunder
Left to tarnish
Perhaps to wither
In their own time

The hazy faces becoming hazier still
The laughter and stories dimming
Ashes blowing
The pyre is cooling
In its own time

I've broken free from gilded fetters
My heart no longer hidden
Not lost but here
To stay a while
In my own time

The tug is fragile and frayed these days
Though a few fierce threads remain
Ideas and choices
Germinate
In my own time

(Hughes, 2010)

The poem gives a sense of time and space for reflection, separating me from my past. The Celtic Queen has laid down her instruments of war (such as my framework and my skills at pragmatic game playing) and is allowing them to tarnish or wither in natural ways. The "hazy faces becoming hazier still" evoke the brevity of past contact with clients and are echoed by the way light, fire and danger from those environments are losing their potency and heat. The "gilded fetters" is a reference to the lucrative but constricting nature of my corporate work and breaking free leaves me in a place where I am "Not lost but here". I may not be clear about my future direction but I am fully present with myself. The last stanza hints at ambivalence towards my past – the ties are now fragile and fraying but not fully broken.

The Magic Flight Home – After a Few Stumbles

If the hero's wish to return to the world is resented by the Gods, then this becomes a lively, often comical pursuit.

(Campbell, 1999: 141)

After my final thesis was submitted, my next hurdle was the viva and I remember that I felt nervous about it. I was struggling with the tension between wanting to get good marks and pass my doctorate (that early determination to cross the finishing line was still very present!) while at the same time wanting to trust myself to stand my ground and believe in my work and approach. I found it a demanding experience – full of insightful observations and probing questions (some of which I managed to answer better than others) and I was relieved and pleased with the verdict of the examining panel – a pass with conditions.

The conditions, written out in a formal letter, meant that I needed to write an additional chapter. So, although I wouldn't describe the final pursuit to the finish line as 'comical', it was certainly 'lively', as I needed to find a final burst of energy to get that additional chapter written. The examiners had thought that there was a lack of engagement with theoretical sources in my thesis and asked that I make them explicit. In particular, I was to make a robust defence of my choice of an autoethnographic methodology within an Action Research paradigm, as there were many in the academic world who were far from convinced that this was a legitimate approach.

Their comments made me realise how complete my conversion to a subjective world-view had been: the efficacy of participatory Action Research seemed so obvious to me, I was surprised I needed to explain its benefits – let alone defend it! I had taken at face value the call for different research approaches as useful additions to scholarly research. Richardson and St. Pierre (2008: 476) say we are "fortunate to be working in a post-modernist climate, a time when a multitude of approaches to knowing and telling exist side by side". Ellis and Bochner (1996: 42) argue that "personal autobiographical modes of writing are vital for knowledge production in the social sciences". Denzin and Lincoln (2008: vii) refer to this as a "quiet methodological revolution" and over the period of my inquiry there seemed both a logic and inevitability in being part of that "revolution". I had written and reflected upon my experiences in robust and disciplined detail and I regarded that to be a legitimate contribution to the field of organisational consulting knowledge. There are few such accounts of consulting work from the perspective of practising consultants, and even fewer by women in the context of commercial organisations. Marsh (2009: 24) claims that such accounts from consultants are rare, as typically "consultants have not subjected their work to such microanalysis".

The prospect of constructing a theoretical examination and defence was at first intimidating (I remember saying to Robin, my tutor, "I am not an academic – I am just an organisational consultant!"). However, I wanted my work to be taken seriously and, in choosing to place myself as central to my research methodology, I accepted that I needed to explain why my approach was valid.

It didn't take me long to discover the full extent of the scepticism within many academic circles. Anderson (2006: 382) claims that although autoethnographic approaches have gained acceptance in qualitative research journals, they remain "marginalised in mainstream social science literature". This was brought home to me when reading Hunt (2009: 1). She says that her autoethnographic writing was deemed "too risky" to be entered into the RAE (Research Assessment Exercise) that took place in British universities in 2008 and "has been advised strongly that in career terms this is not a good way to go". Polkinghorne (2007: 472) points out that "there remain elements of non-acceptance of the reformist efforts". Recent academic federal funding in the US suggests that support for participatory Action Research, and the informing paradigms that give it life, are being questioned. Polkinghorne (2007: 474) observes that there is increasingly "a realist epistemology and a rejection of postmodern approaches in the USA." I was beginning to understand why my examiners required me to make a robust case for my choice.

My head was soon buzzing with what Kemmis and McTaggart (2000: 594) describe as the vitriol associated with the "paradigm wars", where different ontological perspectives collide in a "fertile obsession with validity", as Lather (1993: 673) puts it. Olesen (2000: 215) observes that qualitative researchers have been "patient" in trying to respond to questions of validity, but describes the "absurdity of validity" inherent in a constructionist world-view where there is no one correct interpretation. Despite their misgivings about the notion of validity being misplaced in participatory Action Research, many action researchers responded to the challenge of validity by suggesting criteria by which to assess the validity and quality of the research approach. Denzin and Lincoln (2008: 33) claim that criteria such as "credibility, transferability, dependability and conformity" should replace positivist criteria such as "internal and external validity, reliability and objectivity". Richardson and St. Pierre (2008: 480) suggest four criteria to judge the validity and standard of research – "substantive contribution, aesthetic merit, reflexivity and impact".

Ultimately I took Heron's (1996) encouragement to choose and explain my own elements of validity. The criteria that seem most resonant to me were believability, disciplined methodology, relatability and the intent to continue the discourse with others in the service of practical and useful knowledge. I went on to give evidence of how these qualities informed my work. For example, the idea of believability seemed central to me. The narrative in my thesis had an authentic quality to it as I didn't try to disguise the inherent ambiguity, muddle and uncertainty of my world. So much so that in earlier drafts of my thesis I felt there was too much ambiguity and muddle to be acceptable for public consumption. In attempting to smooth this out and to present a more polished version of myself, I was rightly criticised by my DSG and supervisor for producing something more akin to a client report than autoethnographic research. It was simply not a believable account.

However, there was still something missing from my list. For me, it has been best expressed by Olesen (2000: 394) who observed that "researchers seem to have lost the human, passionate elements of their research". She argues that research requires "passion for people, passion for communication and passion for understanding people." This encouraged me to reframe my final claims to validity and quality by asking a series of questions. Is my work heartfelt, believable and passionate? Were the narratives of my inner world compelling, imaginative and intriguing? Were my conclusions and arguments provocative enough to stimulate further dialogue? Was my work important and significant for the world of organisational consulting?

My final conclusion was to offer these questions as a way to judge the quality of my work and the efficacy of my approach.

The Return and Master of the World – How My Doctoral Work is Sustaining Itself and Informing My Practice

"Live" Nietzsche says "as though the day was here". It is not society that is to guide and save the creative hero, but precisely the reverse...

(Campbell, 1999: 199)

It has been two years since my inquiry formally ended but, in truth, it never really stopped. Judy Marshall (2001) talked about the idea of "living life as inquiry" and this has been the legacy of my doctorate. Although my journaling is less frequent than during my inquiry, it has become an ingrained habit and I find myself applying the discipline of critical subjectivity to many aspects of my life.

I recently joined a creative-writing course to help me get started in writing my first novel. The course was full of techniques and ideas about structure, plot, dialogue and the best ways to find an agent and get published. Whilst all of this was very helpful, I found myself being more interested in understanding my creative process and journaling my reflections. I noticed that the idea of getting published seemed to shut something down inside me (perhaps being too reminiscent of shiny striving). Instead, I am engaged with finding my own voice, learning my craft, paying attention to how I allow my imaginative responses freedom to create a fictional sense of place, character and plot. I notice my patterns of sense making, reflect on my inner dialogue and have even given the central character in my novel a journaling habit of her own, interspersing the action with insights into her own inner complexities.

I re-entered the world of commercial organisations after my six-month sabbatical with a much clearer sense of what constituted meaningful work. One-to-one coaching seemed to offer shelter from the wider toxicity of organisational life and I decided to make this central to my practice. In building up my coaching practice I am not only concerned with finding work but, more significantly, with developing mutual trust and respect. This trust and respect allow both me and my clients to bring all of ourselves into the relationship, so we are working in partnership. This includes being warm and empathic but also having the courage to do some straight talking, if I find myself getting irritated or upset.

In addition to my coaching work, I now actively seek out partnership with other consultants and have reduced the amount of time I work alone. At the heart of my decision to work with others is a concern for mutuality and care between us. This rarely happened when I was more concerned with being independent and had an aura of competitiveness about me.

In the past, I would have accepted work even if I thought it wasn't that meaningful, then fight an uphill battle to have the work adapted. For example, I would agree to design and facilitate a one-off, five-day leadership training programme and then work hard to add ongoing coaching elements and follow-up sessions to ensure the impact of the learning was supported in the participants' real jobs. These days, I have become more comfortable saying "no thanks", rather than start a protracted negotiation to reframe the request. Some of the contractual dynamics in organisations feel so wrong from the outset (for example, taking part in a Request For Proposals) that I no longer participate in them. I turn down an invitation to tender for work or will do it only in a way that feels right for me.

In bringing an increased level of self-awareness and intentionality to my work, I now make thoughtful decisions about what I accept and the organisations I work with. As a result I feel more relaxed, kinder to myself and people experience me as calmer. Paradoxically I suspect my evaluations (when I care to look at them) have not been adversely affected and I find myself with a healthy amount of work.

What about my trust thesis and my commitment to continue the discourse in service of deepening our knowledge about the phenomenon? I do get regular requests to run trust workshops and I am mindful of my intention to continue the dialogue with others. However, I am careful about how I frame my role (I don't get drawn into the 'thought leader' label even though I now have Dr in my title), contracting for a participative approach. I start with a health warning about models and the danger of regarding trust as a phenomenon that can be described as a reification of 'something' (i.e. an experience that could be objectified and delivered). Rather, I suggest a number of questions that encourage the group to explore the nature of the phenomenon, in the context they find themselves in. In this way, I think people come to regard trust as a quality of relating and one that is complex, dynamic, elusive and organic in its development. It changes with every gesture, in every thought, in every context. Once this is understood, trust is often reframed as an aspirational quality of relating that might never actually be achieved, but is worth striving towards.

I suspect that I will always be working towards the aspiration of trusting myself and working towards creating trusting relationships. For now, the best professional context for that seems to be working one to one with people, somewhat in the background. I have also extended the contexts I work with beyond the commercial. I coach headteachers within the private and public education sectors and am an active trustee of a charity – supporting vulnerable children in Northern Namibia. At many levels, professionally and personally, my inquiry has had a profound impact on my life in a positive way.

However, I don't want to give the impression I have found some Holy Grail of spiritual enlightenment. I worry when others talk of the redemption that comes with deepening self-awareness. Some of my colleagues can come across as evangelists and their certainty troubles me. I think when you are concerned about understanding ideas such as trust, that sort of certainty might prevent you from holding complexity. The essence of my practice now is about how I am alive and awake to the complexity within me, in my relationships with others and within the phenomenon of trust itself.

CHAPTER 4

A Dialogue about Self-reflexivity and Holding Environments

John and I had been reflecting on Heifetz's assertion that adaptive change requires learning and a safe enough holding environment. I suggested that learning is a change process too, which lead us to muse about the profound challenges the four-year-long, intensive first-person inquiry on ADOC presents for participants and supervisors alike. We dive into this conversation with our response to Jennifer's chapter.

Kathleen: Jennifer's research is a lovely example of how self-reflexivity can be profoundly disturbing and at the same time makes you stronger. As a young girl Jennifer had learned that others could make decisions about her life without consulting her and that it was her responsibility to make the best of it and not disappoint grown-ups. As is often the case with potent introjections (unexamined social rules or norms), this rule had arisen in a very particular moment and context but had been carried across different contexts over time; it was seriously impairing Jennifer's ability to develop her agency, her voice. As she started to reclaim her power and dislodge this particular introjection, she began to see its impact in all sorts of situations. Once she had disrupted it in one context, other areas of her life followed. However, she avoids the temptation to replace one all encompassing rule with another. Rather than moving from being voiceless to being vociferous at all times, she chooses wisely and carefully when to voice her disquiet and when to desist.

John: I think her chapter illustrates beautifully an adaptive change in process. I can't imagine the courage Jennifer must have brought to her research given the charged experiences that enforced her introjections. How did she manage to keep going?

Kathleen: It was not easy, for her and those of us who were alongside her, but Jennifer was very determined. With hindsight, I think her first years on ADOC of furious reading and writing papers, quoting 'learned scholars', but somehow remaining invisible in the text, was a kind of defence against anxiety in its own right. At the time, I hadn't quite realised that, because I wasn't aware of the depth and sometimes hair-raising nature of the work that Jennifer was poised to embark on.

John: I can see the importance of a good holding environment for anyone engaging in this level of adaptive work. Could you say more about how that is configured on ADOC, as I sense what is done on ADOC to achieve a good holding environment is an experience of direct relevance to the wider world – of non-academic organisations?

Kathleen: We aim to establish a genuine community of practice, learning and research. There are a series of workshops, led by faculty and later also by participants, during which we explore the principles and practices of Action Research. We pay attention to group dynamics and issues of power and participation as they arise. But it is especially the smaller supervision groups, with four or five participants and a supervisor, that offer a safe context. The change doctors often refer to the importance of their supervision group for working through the most challenging moments and staying on course.

John: I see the significance and the value of peer learning on ADOC within an intimate and facilitated setting. I imagine the role of a supervisor in this context can be quite challenging? You are joining what is in some ways a peer learning group, and at the same time you have a different responsibility: holding academic and professional standards, as well as staying focussed on the reflexive work. Noticing, appraising and containing all at the same time.

Kathleen: I find it challenging and exhilarating in equal measure, although not necessarily both at the same time. [Laughs] Although we all have a personal style and approach, I think there are common threads. I sometimes liken supervision to parenting. It is similar in that we seek to support participants in pursuing their personal growth challenge, with the expectation that at some stage they will out-grow us. Fletcher (1999) argues that this requires relational skills such as being aware of and paying attention to one's own and others' emotional reality, empathy, vulnerability and self-reflection. More importantly, it requires a whole way of thinking and approach that is not commonly associated with (academic) development or training programmes, but with the private, family sphere. She considers relational work an occasion for growth for both parties, another similarity with parenting in my view. I have dug out a quote: "The essence of mutual vulnerability, mutual openness, and mutual influence is reciprocity – an expectation that the other will be motivated to minimise status differences, to foster growth-in-connection interactions, to respond to and recognise the inevitability of vulnerability and mutual dependence. This mutuality is antithetical to achieving pre-ordained goals. By its very nature, the outcomes of mutual interaction are fluid, unknowable – the essence of creativity rather than management by objectives" (Fletcher, 1999: 114). It is precisely this notion of mutual growth that is lost in organisations, when relational activity and skills – much like trust, as we argued earlier – become instrumentalised. In the process they lose their transformational potential.

John: So if I get this, as faculty you are joining the ADOC community of peer learning and practice from a stance of mutuality. That involves reducing power differentials, being willing to be changed by your engagement with participants, being open and vulnerable?

Kathleen: Yes, all of that. One of the consequences also is a level of unpredictability, always tricky in an academic context, or in any change context for that matter. We are back to the idea of certainty and predictability. Dealing with what is happening right here, right now, rather than to stay doggedly on a predetermined course, can be scary as well as the only sensible thing to do. [Laughs]

John: And how do you square all of the mutuality and fluidity with the considerable constraints of an academic context?

Kathleen: That is a difficult balancing act. Not only do we need to continually remind participants of the academic criteria they need to meet, we also need to judge their work. It can be a very uncomfortable experience.

John: I can see similarities with the challenges for leaders and change agents we talked about in our previous dialogue. There are always constraints to be taken into account and difficult decisions to be made. This notion of 'growth in connection' with all that it entails, seems to me, much like proper trust, a far cry from the kind of relating that prevails in organisations. Are we concluding that it's not possible to create a safe holding environment in organisations?

Kathleen: Probably. I do think we are saying that creating a good enough holding environment is a real challenge, and also that keeping power differentials as small as can be is an important aspect of that. It doesn't mean that we pretend we're all in the same boat: we mostly aren't. But it does mean that we remain alert to how we take up our role and our power, and the impact it has on those around us…

John: …and notice how our own defences impact on others? Doesn't that imply that a change agent may want to seek good holding too?

Kathleen: Absolutely. ADOC supervisors have their own supervision, and I believe it is crucial for change agents also, and that includes managers and leaders. Holding of the holders… let's go find out how Jennifer Carlston is now holding her clients.

CHAPTER 5

Finding Voice, Giving Voice, Shaping Voice

By Jennifer Carlson

Introducing Jennifer Carlson

A mere 250 words feels brief for the explanation of a point of view as well as a body of work, so I will be direct in my introduction. I have been drawn into the question of how change happens since attempting to try new business practices early in my career, only to be met with scorn and resistance despite evidence of success. This taught me the power of culture and what happens when groups band together under common views and beliefs.

I spent several years working from a behaviourist perspective: that is, I believed that people could be guided into new patterns of work through reason and order. Modest but very short-lived success at this showed me that emotions – be it anxiety or safety – trump anything the logical mind can conceive.

I defined relationships as behaving like the people around me, in order to fit in and influence change. I failed miserably at instituting anything of real significance and realised several things from these experiences: that denying myself means denying my existence, and in particular my womanhood; that being in relation with someone is about walking a very fine and precious line between empathy and forthrightness; and that it takes courage to stay true to that line.

In my work today I seek to recognise and appreciate where people are starting from, and then find ways to move with them in a direction that reflects aspirations as well as the creation of value. It is never easy, always unexpected and sometimes terrifying. But it is work that I wholeheartedly pursue.

* * * * *

So here I am, seeing the cycle continue over three decades later as I consider how I, too, was a young woman, full of energy, and was ultimately driven out (and worse) because I also 'didn't fit in'. So I feel an even stronger sense of urgency, I fret at the massive noise in the system and I hope, ultimately, that I can be heard over the din.

Taking on the challenge of a doctoral degree is not a casual commitment. It's many years in the making and, within that, consists of a multitude of silent hours surrounded by books and articles, often lit by the glow of a computer. To maintain the needed motivation and persistence, it helps to have a compelling mission, a curiosity to pursue a certain insight or to achieve a particularly lofty goal. My doctoral pursuit, though, didn't start that way. I didn't have a clear idea of what I wanted to do, I didn't have a research topic and I didn't even have a particular problem or challenge I wished to wrestle with. Instead, it started with a vague but pronounced feeling of unease about my work, a sense that despite success as an organisation consultant, I was somehow missing the point of the whole thing. It was as if I had been nibbling around the edges of my clients' problems from behind a shield of safety and, as a result, getting nowhere. Even worse, I couldn't even blame it on circumstances or the boundary of my assignments. Rather, I was feeling complicit with my clients in avoiding the source of our shared concerns, as if we were acting out a parody of work, instead of digging in and doing something of real value.

With this hazy foundation, my first months of doctoral work were meandering at best, as I struggled to find something to grab hold of. And while the central themes of my research did not emerge for several more years, I soon knew that it would be linked to some early work experiences that had left me frustrated, angry and traumatised, concerns that I had theoretically 'forgotten' but in truth had stayed far too close to the surface of my life.

I am now considering the fact that it has taken me nearly two hours to write these few words, and that they are as vague and unfocused as my initial research pursuits. So I will attempt to sum things up squarely and directly. The work experiences I am referring to began with my first job out of college, where as a young woman I was a supervisor in a manufacturing plant and as such lived in an environment rife with sexual harassment. It was emotionally and psychologically debilitating as I tried to create a career foothold in a world that felt alien to me, and one in which my colleagues preferred that I fail rather than violate their unspoken culture, which had a decidedly male orientation.

To escape the frustrations and my sense of personal failure, I left and accepted a completely different position as a teacher at a private school for developmentally disabled adults. I believed that I was now entering a safe role, in which as a teacher I would leave the gendered environment behind and commit to something that had far more value than making machinery parts. However, only weeks after my new career began, I was raped by one of the students and, perhaps worse, blamed for placing myself in such a position and not sufficiently defending myself. Happy to have survived but utterly confused by the messages I was receiving, I shoved the emotional aftermath deep inside and created new opportunities for myself, which included not just what ultimately became my career as an organisation consultant, but also a life as a wife and mother of two wonderful children.

These experiences, though, which started as a backdrop to my doctoral research, soon became figural for me. The midpoint of my studies centred on understanding what happened, why it happened, and how it influenced who I was and what I did. It was a profound influence on my work to become an organisational consultant (which armed me to gain a deep insight on group and leadership behaviour) but it also weighed on me in a variety of professional settings. In particular, I came to recognise that one stream of anxiety for me was in small-group work, a bread-and-butter component of any consultant's practice.

I had known for a long time that I avoided (but couldn't completely dismiss) small-group facilitation and that, when in dialogue, my preferred style was to let others take the lead so I could listen quietly. I contributed when I needed to, but with anxiety and only as a last resort. I started to spot other aspects of my work where anxiety showed up and, after peeling back layer after layer of understanding, I finally decided to frame my initial research interests around the idea of courage. Perhaps by embracing courage in all its forms, I could marshal what I needed to face down my demons and be the kind of consultant I wanted to be.

The concept of courage soon evolved into a particular point of view which I refer to as 'feminine courage'. As I explored courage, I identified with fellow researchers who noted that the more commonly socialised view of courage had a decidedly masculine perspective. This was a testosterone-laced view of courage in battle or of rescuing victims, who most often were women. While I could identify with the need for, and practice of, courage in my life, I longed for a better way to embrace it; and thus I shifted the lens and began to look at what a feminised view of courage might be like.

As I pursued this line of thought, I found two prongs for my reflection. The first was that courage for me has a relational nature. Bakan (1996) put forth the notion that men and women tend to show up in the world as agentic or communal. Agency refers to the concept in which a person has a strong individual orientation. He describes agency as "self-protection, self-assertion and self-expansion... and the urge to master." In the context of career pursuits, Plunkett (2001) describes it as "the existence of a clear goal, strategy, and unflagging ambition." Bakan notes that men tend to be socialised to act from an agentic perspective.

In contrast, women are more in communion or communal – or are socialised to be so. According to Bakan, communion is "the participation of the individual in some larger organism of which the individual is a part." Further, it manifests itself as "being at one with other organisms" and is characterised as "contact, openness and union", as well as "noncontractual cooperation". As I reflected on this, I recognised a significant lack of agency on my part in a variety of organisational settings and a particularly strong communal orientation. I felt safest when I didn't assert myself (if you're not seen or heard, then maybe predators won't know you exist) and also when I became one with the group, as being in relation with others diminished the likelihood that they might turn on me. In addition, it's hard to hold space with agency and communion simultaneously; asserting oneself may break some valued bonds. Looking at these concepts through the lens of courage led me to conclude that feminine courage is required to take action that honours one's own needs, especially if it means rupturing relationships.

Through Action Research and the use of narrative approaches such as autoethnography, I could see this thread of anxiety and reluctance to fully engage framing my presence in group settings. Yet, this was still only half of the story. The pursuit of safety came at the cost of my voice – and not just my literal voice, but the very essence of who I was and what I believed. Each time I sat silently, I had a perspective about how I showed up in the world that remained unsaid. And over time, without my voice being put out there during times that mattered most to me, I was relegating myself to inexistence.

I acknowledge that I backed into this trap honestly. I learned through the harassment and abuse I'd experienced early in my career that it wasn't safe to step up and work in ways that ran counter to existing practices and beliefs. And in fact, my silence was also an antidote for the post-traumatic stress syndrome that I had unknowingly been suffering under for the past twenty years. But to sort it all out and to begin expressing my voice, I'd need actively to practice feminine courage.

As my doctoral research wrapped up, I was grappling with the extent to which I had given in to silence. Not only had I avoided some of the more difficult problems within my clients' organisations, I had also stayed silent through an emotionally abusive marriage. Ultimately, that year became a series of endings for me: I concluded my thesis, I ended my marriage and I left the consulting organisation I'd been a part of for over twenty years to strike out on my own as an independent consultant.

I am now nearly two full years past that transition point and, while my formal research has concluded, my exploration and pursuit of feminine courage has not. This chapter will therefore put a lens on what has transpired since that time and, in particular, examine how feminine courage and finding my voice have made an impact on how I pursue my work.

Coming Full Circle

Nearly a year after I had established my consulting practice, I received a call from a former colleague who I'll call 'Aaron'. He'd been asked by a client to do an analysis of their training function – how they developed and executed learning programs for new employees, as well as training that was conducted when new products were launched. The goal was to identify strategies that would elevate their capabilities in order to take them to 'best in class'. Was I interested in partnering with him?

Aaron sought me out because part of my organisational expertise is in the area of developing tailored learning programs. I'd often worked with large corporations who had outsourced the design and development of learning initiatives, leaving their internal staff to focus on managing projects and executing delivery. I had developed many such programs over the years and brought more than just research and analysis skills to the project. The project goal alone was enough to pique my interest, but what I found particularly intriguing was that it happened to be for the same company that I had worked for when I got out of college – the same company in which I had been subject to sexual harassment more than twenty-five years earlier. Being asked to scrutinise how the organisation supported new employees as they transitioned into the business held an irony I couldn't pass up.

The irony actually extended even further. Not only had my client company (which I'll refer to as 'Manufacturing Co') shaped my view of life in the world of business, I had also briefly held a position in their training department before I left the company. My assumption was that business practices had changed many times over since that time, but the extent and the specifics of the change were completely unknown to me and therefore held a particular curiosity. As I considered the possibilities, it gave me an odd sense of time travel, as if this project would allow me to see what my life would look like now if I had chosen a different path.

Aaron and I were partnered with the client, who I'll call 'Kurt', and together the three of us started conducting interviews of stakeholders and subject-matter experts, as well as examining third-party data. It didn't take long to see why the project was initiated, as there were issues everywhere we looked. For example, there was no attention given to the learner's needs: instead it was believed that any learning solution would do. Cheaper was considered better, even if it meant that the resulting training program didn't have the desired impact. The only measurement system in place was designed to justify all prior decisions. And the closer we looked, the worse it got.

As the problems piled up I became anxious about the extent of the situation. I could find absolutely nothing to give praise to and the list of faults seemed to go on forever. Could it really be this bad? I wondered briefly if my personal history with Manufacturing Co was influencing the data I was looking at, but I quickly realised that those thoughts were merely a smoke screen and an invitation for denial. For me the question started to become: did I have the courage to speak the truth as I saw it – and would leadership at Manufacturing Co, starting with Kurt, have the courage to hear it?

The extent of my struggle finally revealed itself a few days later. The three of us were working through list after list of problems, trying to understand what had gone wrong, when the conversation shifted to the team responsible for the training we were examining. This team was clearly central to the situation. The dilemma we were facing was that the group that worked in the training department was a bit of an enigma to us because they were not among those we interviewed. While we had been given carte blanche to do the research as we saw fit, there had been one significant exception: our work had to be conducted 'under the radar', which meant that we had to do it without the participation of the current training team. The reason given for this was that they would throw up resistance and slow down progress, especially if a group of outsiders stormed their gates. And while this made a small amount of sense, it also struck me as both wrong and odd – but wrong and odd in a way that was ripe with meaning. What was being kept from us?

As we continued to talk, Aaron and Kurt shared a few informal stories they had heard about the department that for now I will simply describe as revealing its members to be quirky, aggressive and unpredictable. And as they chatted, I suddenly saw clarity within the mess we were facing. We were staring at a much more complex and systemic situation than a problematic training department. The training group was a symptom of a larger situation related to a regressive and insular leadership culture that acted out of convenience instead of purpose. Essentially, the training department consisted of people who had failed elsewhere in the organisation: rather than make the hard decisions relating to counselling and dismissing poor performers, a place had been created in which to put them. This group was the "training team". The reason I knew this with certainty was because it had been the practice in Manufacturing Co twenty-five years earlier, when I was a part of training. Back then, I had unwittingly raised my hand to gain what I thought would be valuable career experience. It wasn't until I was in the role that I realised, based on first-hand experience with incompetent peers, that I had got more than I'd bargained for. So there I sat, staring at not just the net result of dysfunction but the result of *decades* of dysfunction.

These conclusions felt like much more than I had been asked to identify and report on and led me to consider whether or not I had the courage to name what I was seeing, as I saw many risks. For example, the reason Kurt was asked to lead this research project was because he'd been the leader of the training team in another operating group. If I explained to him that the training department was a dumping ground for failed employees, would I be insulting him in the process? I wondered also if I'd established sufficient credibility to bear the weight of such a statement, along with all the other problems we'd identified... would it turn into a 'who-do-you-think-you-are' response? And would Aaron and other colleagues feel I'd betrayed them if I presented conclusions that angered their clients at Manufacturing Co?

One thing that struck me, as I weighed my alternatives, was that part of the reason the situation existed was because leadership at Manufacturing Co lacked institutional courage. Dismissing people was difficult to do, as it is in any company; but Manufacturing Co also had, and continues to have, a reputation for providing lifetime employment. It was exceedingly rare for someone to be made redundant and even then it was usually due to gross legal or ethical violations. So to sack someone for poor performance took a level of effort – of courage – that just wasn't done. These thoughts, in turn, made me think about my own courage. If I opted for a safer way around the situation, wouldn't I simply be falling into old patterns in which I 'nibbled at the edges of problems'? This didn't sit well with me and pushed me to be forthright and begin to share my opinions, and thus my voice.

Using my beliefs that courage would emerge more steadfastly if I paid attention to relationships, I tested out my concerns with Aaron and then others on the team, leaving Kurt for last. After each conversation, I had a better grasp of my perspective and of the words that would allow for some challenging conversations, but within a reasonable boundary. I then approached Kurt and, as I shared my thoughts, I was relieved to find less resistance than I had anticipated on his part. Since he hadn't met the training department yet, he wasn't entirely convinced my statements were correct, but I could tell he was putting 'two and two together' with data points of his own.

Aaron, Kurt and I went on to finalise the research, which included a struggle to find the language for the final report that would describe what we had learned through the entire project. With my leadership and cultural concerns as the biggest example, we weighed how best to convey a raft of bad news in a way that would allow it to be heard. We ultimately decided to share all the conclusions we'd reached, including my primary concern, but we shaded things slightly in the interest of passing this first hurdle. If we didn't get sufficient agreement to secure funding, any opportunity for improvement would be lost.

As I reflect back, this was certainly not the toughest challenge I've faced through my consulting career, and I wonder a bit why I felt so strongly about needing courage to follow it through. I believe part of it was due to the feelings I was harbouring from my early experiences, which made the episode even larger than it was in the moment. I also did not feel I was on firm ground relationally: I wasn't yet sure I had earned the respect I needed to convey harsh truths. But there is also a catch in that regard – earning the right to speak forthrightly often comes as a result of doing so. Therefore, there is an open space that must be stepped into in order to create the needed ground.

In the end, the report was well received and agreements to take action were reached across all stakeholders. Budgets were established and Kurt was given a new assignment to lead the redesign of the internal training organisation. Aaron went on to another project and I was asked to stay on and collaborate with Kurt to implement the changes we had recommended. Recognising the mountain ahead of us, he got approval for the full-time funding of four new staff members. And so it happened that I essentially became, once again, a member of Manufacturing Co.

One Foot In and One Foot Out

The day they handed me my key card and parking pass for Manufacturing Co was not a good one for me. I wasn't an employee – I was a consultant on contract – yet I would be acting like an employee: I had a desk to work at and full access to the facility and everyone on the team. My concerns with this ranged from wanting to work from the comfort of my own home office to anxiety about the culture I was entering. Based on what I'd learned through the research, I had suspicions about how much the organisation had actually changed during the past decades. But more importantly, even if it hadn't, had I changed enough to do more than tolerate – or run away – from what I'd encounter?

The answer to my question about what had changed came quickly and it was clear that the gendered environment I'd left was still intact. On a basic level, there were far fewer women than men and the majority of leadership positions were also held by men. But there was also an agentic, aggressive perspective on how people communicated and how work got done. Perhaps the most striking example of the masculine culture, and the acceptance of it, came during my first week. A few meetings were organised so that those of us who were new could become acquainted with the team. I was in a meeting with several people, including George (not his real name) who had been in the department for several years. He was among those who were described as "quirky" and it wasn't long before I learned what that meant. George provided some personal background on his career, during which he noted that he had once worked for a particular woman (who, having been in a senior position, had left several years earlier to join another company). As he mentioned this, he added, "And I have to tell you, I didn't like 'Carol' at all. In fact, this is what I thought of her." He then noted that he had a stuffed doll in his office and that when her name came up, he would hit the doll repeatedly against his desk. As he explained this to us, he demonstrated his actions in pantomime, complete with a vigorous hitting motion, as well as a string of insults, all directed at the Carol doll.

My reaction as I watched this was one of both disbelief and disappointment.

This kind of behaviour was acceptable? Those in the room who worked with him simply rolled their eyes and gently shook their heads, as they had seen his show a number of times. So clearly this was not a charade designed exclusively for us, but rather his typical exhibition. But his tirade against women – and an especially violent one at that – did not sit well with me at all. (I will add that he later repeated his demonstration for me, but this time with the actual doll. When he was done, all I could think to say was, "Don't you think it's time you retired that doll? After all, Carol hasn't worked here for several years." At which point, I walked away. I haven't seen the doll since, but it isn't as if the culture has changed, either.)

My role on the project is to design training programs that will improve the productivity and effectiveness of their employee network. But if I can change the culture at the same time, I will.

Finding Moments of Courage

The project got underway and, as we'd suspected, we uncovered many more opportunities for change. The volume of concerns and the overall scope of the initiative made progress exceedingly slow; however, after six months we were finally in the midst of an opportunity to demonstrate to the organisation how we could activate the new learning strategies and tactics that so far we had only been talking about.

The opportunity came about as a result of a series of organisational changes and business improvements that led to the need to hire eighty entry-level employees for a front-line role. They hadn't done any hiring of this significance in a long time and there was a lot of excitement around the decision. Naturally, this new group of people would require training and I was given responsibility for determining the learning strategy and designing the resulting program.

The job role for the new employees was quite complex and ultimately resulted in the design of a five-week training program. This in turn required the participation of over 150 people as subject-matter experts, content developers, project managers and more. Any desire I might have had to toil quietly in the background was never a possibility.

As work progressed, it became clear that there was more than just idle curiosity about what we were doing. I could feel an underlying tension about our work and why we were doing it, as well as subtle comments that suggested 'we'd better get it right'. Consequently, I found myself in numerous meetings in which I tried to explain the strategy and design, and especially in a way that would alleviate any concerns. These were always tricky because the learning was experiential and thus any description offered was essentially a one-dimensional version of a three-dimensional experience. (It's like trying to explain a Shakespeare play using sock puppets.) By the end of each meeting, everyone seemed comfortable and our work would continue unabated. Yet the underlying tension never seemed to diminish: I'd soon find myself in another design review, having to explain things all over again.

This continued in a similar vein until about ten days before our launch. Once again, I was given notice to conduct a design review, this time with a group of top executives (directors and VPs) I'd met with a few weeks earlier. During the previous meeting we'd gone through everything in detail, they'd given me their input, and plans were revised accordingly. Now they apparently had more questions and, as we were near the eleventh hour, I was hopeful it was nothing of real consequence.

Kurt joined me at the meeting, although we agreed I'd take the lead since I was much closer to the content. We gave a quick status report to the assembled group but it wasn't long before the questions started coming at us. Most of them were from Rita, who had missed a couple of meetings. She had an assertive, rat-a-tat-tat style and she peppered me with a variety of issues. Some of her questions were on topics we'd dealt with previously, which were quickly addressed, but others related to a personal agenda of issues. Tensions began to escalate and soon you could see doubt creeping into the conversation.

It was at this point that Paul, who had been fairly quiet so far, jumped in. He held up the learning agenda and began stabbing his finger at it. "This doesn't make any sense! Why would you teach it this way? No-one will learn anything!"

As he started to talk, I could feel my anger growing. It felt like I was facing two bullies on a playground and they were feeding off of each other. I was also mad because, whilst none of what they said was true, I also knew that it was my word against theirs. I wouldn't have proof until we conducted the training, but if I didn't get things under control, I'd never get my chance. So when it was quickly clear that Paul wasn't going to shut up, I decided to jump in and cut him off.

"Excuse me, excuse me," I said, yet he kept going. And since he wasn't stopping, then neither would I. "You're misunderstanding" I said, my voice raised higher, trying to talk over him. "That's not true... you've missed the point..." Finally, after what felt like an eternity, he stopped. And when he did, I leapt into the void.

"Let me start by explaining that every word in this document was written with the learner in mind," I said, pointing my own finger at the papers in his hand. "It is absolutely imperative that they leave prepared to do their job, and careful attention has been given to every aspect of their experience..." Beyond these few words, I have no memory of my comments, but I do know I went on for several minutes, describing the vision and emphasising key points in the strategy.

When I finally got done, the room was quiet for a moment, and then Rita spoke up. "All of this makes sense, and it looks like you've got some good plans underway. I just have a couple more things, and then I have to run..." The meeting wrapped up a few minutes later, which was when some self-doubt hit me, accompanied by a small wave of anxiety. Was it really smart of me to get into a shouting match with a senior executive?

But even with the rush of anxiety, I also had a shock of awareness as I recognised how out-of-character it was for me to go on the offensive. As I described at the opening of this chapter, I have been fighting my own natural tendencies to hide my voice and let others carry conversations, especially strong ones. Yet there I was, finding the courage to go toe-to-toe with two of the more hard-core executives in the organisation. I may have created other problems by breaking rank, but it was with a certain sense of accomplishment.

Since then, I have reflected more on what was different at that time. A thought I have been considering this past year is that courage is more accessible to me now that I'm consulting on my own, and that the word 'independent' actually holds a lot of power for me. I have never taken the relationships I have with my colleagues lightly, and acting as a good team member is a big part of how I show up in my work. But I'm beginning to realise that being a team player has been a big inhibitor in how I contribute. More than I realised, I often carry multiple voices in my head as I work to balance the needs of the various people I feel accountable to. It becomes particularly tricky as situations become complex and, as a consequence, I tend to defer my opinion if it means keeping the peace. With just me showing up for the job, there is no 'peace to be kept' and no boss to please. Subsequently, I believe it has freed me up to express myself more authentically. If I fail, it's on me and no-one else. And if what I do has negative consequences, I also find that the pain of hurting others is harder to bear than self-inflicted wounds.

Validation for a Relational View of Courage

The program launched successfully; everything went as planned and the few problems that cropped up were all anticipated in advance and quickly resolved. The organisational curiosity that we had experienced continued but transitioned to a 'viral buzz' which actually swept across the US (as people were passing along comments that they had heard from others). Besides the chatter, we were also getting drop-in visitors throughout each day. Apparently, some people needed to see for themselves what was really happening. By week's end we started calling the class 'The Circus', since the show appeared to be in town.

Kurt checked in with me, the project team and the class on several occasions and, by all accounts, he seemed pleased with how well everything was going. I know he had his own hopes for success, partially because of the high visibility but also because it was the first real test of our new plans. It may have been a few drops in the ocean of change we were swimming in, but as the first few they were welcome drops indeed.

When the week wrapped, I stuck my head into Kurt's office to say goodbye and to offer my own sigh of relief that we'd made it through the week. He thanked me for the work I'd put in, then surprised me by asking if I had time to go out for a drink. We weren't an after-hours crowd, so this was atypical, but I assumed he had an agenda that was more appropriate for an off-site conversation. I agreed and we quickly made plans.

No sooner had I said 'yes' and returned to my desk to close down for the day, than I felt a rush of anxiety. Was there actually bad news to share – had something happened I wasn't aware of? Conversely, even if it was good news, that made me uncomfortable too. I typically don't like being the centre of attention, as it tends to provoke feelings of vulnerability in me rather than the pleasure others get from it. Over time, I've identified it as just one of the side effects of my post-traumatic stress disorder; and it's a contributor to my reluctance to speaking up in groups. I sometimes refer to it as "hiding in plain sight" – if I don't draw attention to myself, then it can help keep bad things from happening to me. Yet my internal turmoil still didn't match up with the situation. I was hyper alert and it was all I could do to maintain a calm and studied composure.

It was several days before I sorted out how I felt in those moments, but I ultimately determined that the scrutiny had unexpectedly escalated into feeling preyed upon. Willingly going to an unknown location with someone – a man – I didn't know that well landed on me like an enormous threat. When these waves hit me, especially if they're unexpected, they always defy logic; I had absolutely no reason to be concerned at any level about accepting his invitation. Yet I know from experience that I can't reason the emotions away and the triggers can be varied. This time it took about 36 hours to shake off the intense emotions, so it didn't stay with me too long; but I share this as a backdrop for how I was feeling during the conversation that took place about an hour later.

We walked a couple of blocks to a local pub, making small talk about family and weekend plans, but the whole time I kept wondering when we'd get to the real conversation. When we walked in, I picked a table near the door, we ordered drinks and soon the dialogue shifted to work. He talked a bit about the week but mostly the focus was on the many problems we still faced. For example, all the training courses – hundreds of them – needed to be redesigned. The team we inherited had limited skills and were sometimes struggling with the pace of change, yet he wasn't in a position to replace them. Leadership was often caught up in the daily business and the numbers, leaving it unable slow down long enough to address strategic issues which, in turn, got in the way of our ability to produce quality work.

Kurt didn't want to talk in order to complain, though. He wanted to get at the heart of the matter and figure out the kinds of actions that needed to happen in order to create the kind of change that we'd been envisioning for nearly a year. Which is when he hit me with an unexpected comment.

> I look at you, and I see the courage you have to step up and take on some really tough challenges. It's as if you're able to stand apart from our culture, see things that the rest of us can't, and then you dive in and do what has to be done. You're not trapped by what your boss is going to say, or the stupid system we're in. You just get in there and do it.

I was completely stunned by what he shared. I felt a small thrill of excitement – he called me courageous! But there was also a sense of exposure, that he'd uncovered something about me that I thought was my secret alone. I don't speak of courage in conversation. I've guarded my dissertation and avoided sharing it with others as I've never been sure of the reaction I'd get or if I was ready for the conversations it might start. Yet here he was, telling me I had courage.

I couldn't look him in the eye as I tried to process his remarks. I stared at the table, trying to listen, but my thoughts took a new turn. *"He must know,"* I thought. *"I must have told him about my thesis. He has to know I'm still doing some writing about courage…"* So in that moment, although I was tempted to just smile, nod and let the conversation keep going on its own, I instead took hold of it myself. I looked up and asked, "Have I ever told you the topic of my doctoral dissertation?" His look of confusion was the answer I needed. "Ummm…

well, you may have told me, but I can't remember right now…" It was exactly what I wanted to hear. He wasn't picking up on verbal cues I had given him. Rather, he had observed actions on my part and independently labelled them as "courageous". He could have chosen any number of words to describe what he saw in me: politically savvy, strategic, thoughtful, committed. But he didn't. He chose the word "courage".

I didn't want to derail the direction he was headed in with our dialogue, so I gave only a brief explanation of my thesis topic and its importance to me. But as we talked I could see that he was using this as a springboard for understanding how he might act differently. This in turn answered the question I was still harbouring about why we were sitting in a bar and not back at the office. He was interested in a coaching conversation and the ability to speak more candidly about topics that were challenging for him (as well as the team), for which an environment like the pub offered a better opportunity.

Before I share the conclusion of our conversation, I also want to add that he, too, had identified the relational aspect I had seen in my courageous actions. It was clear to him that my independence and lack of direct ties to the organisation played an important part in my actions, and he wanted me to maintain that stance because he saw it as valuable to him and to the work that we were doing.

The rest of the discussion became more personal. We talked about what motivates us in our work and, as part of that, I shared some early stories from when I worked for Manufacturing Co in the 1980s. This led to a discussion on culture as well as some questions on his part about where he might have opportunities to improve his performance. That bit included turning the lens of courage on him. (He denied acting courageously, but I was able to give him some really rich examples of when he was.)

After about an hour, we'd had our fill and wrapped things up. While walking down the street, he said, "You know, I say things to you that I don't share with the rest of the team." I interpreted this as being a direct request to keep the conversation between us but, more importantly, I also heard him say that he trusted me enough to share things that felt risky to him. All of which took courage on his part.

* * * * *

Thinking About the 'Carol Doll'

As part of the cycle of reflection, I shared my writing with my doctoral colleagues who had many questions and comments. The most striking aspect of our conversation revolved around what I'd initially thought of as a rather minor part of the overall piece, the story of the 'Carol Doll'.

When I originally wrote the story, I knew I wanted to include the Carol Doll somewhere as it was a startling moment for me that I felt amplified and clarified how I felt about the organisation's culture. In one short encounter, I could illustrate what I was experiencing; words alone couldn't quite capture what was often subtle and implicit. In my first attempt to describe the conversation, I included several emotive and personally situated statements. For example, I described how this badly beaten doll looked to me; her frequent thrashings resulted in a large tear in her neck that to my eyes "looked as if her throat had been slashed." I also added a few words that made clear my feelings of confusion, annoyance, anxiety and threat. But upon further editing, I found myself wanting to take all the 'colour commentary' out and merely paint a dispassionate picture of what happened, thus allowing the readers to decide for themselves what they thought of it. At the time, I was telling myself that it made for a better story for the reader in its stripped-down state but now, I believe there was more going on in how I wrote about it, which I will address shortly.

Getting back to the discussion with my colleagues, the Carol Doll elicited many remarks, most of which centred on the theme of "casual violence". Without really intending to, by simply laying the story out for others to see (which I later described as tossing a strange object into the middle of the room, then scurrying away to watch how people reacted to it) I had painted an even more vivid cultural image than I had realised. Words to describe how they felt seemed hard to come by, so people sought other explanations. One person went to the Internet and pulled up 'Bunny with a head wound'.

There was also a discussion in which broad comparisons were made to filmmakers David Lynch and Quentin Tarantino; that is, the Carol Doll story conveyed a quality of surreal violence that was jarring and difficult to process. The Quentin Tarantino remark struck a chord with me, as I have made it a practice to avoid his work ever since I attempted – but failed – to watch *Pulp Fiction*. *Pulp Fiction* had been out for quite some time before I finally got curious enough to see what all the excitement was about. The small bits I'd heard about it didn't make me think it was my kind of movie, but one Saturday afternoon I had a 'why not?' moment and decided to rent it. My memory now, years later, is a loop of a few seconds of the film. It is early in the movie and John Travolta has just shot a man who is in the trunk of his car. I don't recall the specifics of the dialogue, but the casual, slightly humorous, annoyed behaviour on Travolta's part as he shot bullet after bullet into the body were sufficiently jarring to me that I reached over and turned it off. That scene is now a reference point for me when I select movies to watch; if I sense a *Pulp Fiction*-like quality to it, it remains unseen. And yet here I was, years later, having written something of a comparative nature.

51

It felt good to hear the lively dialogue and comments, which at the time I interpreted as the pleasure that comes from praise and attention. But as I turned this over in my mind, I realised that it was less about being pleased and more about feeling a sense of relief, because resting alongside my own annoyance and anxiety was also a shroud of doubt, which emerged in part from what I omitted in the story. I wasn't the only witness to the beating of the Carol Doll – there were others sitting alongside me. And while I was feeling tacitly threatened, others were feeling entertained. What I saw as being grossly inappropriate, others saw as commonplace. In fact, when I asked about it afterwards ("What do you think of the Carol Doll? Does it bother you at all?") I was often met with things like amusement: "I think it's kind of funny"; dismissiveness: "That's just his way"; or defensive denial: "He's actually a really smart guy". By writing the story of the Carol Doll in the way that I did – without my emotions foregrounded in it – I could offer the experience in its raw state to others and gauge how their reactions were similar to or different from mine. And when the commentary of my colleagues echoed my own perspective, it helped me dispel the nagging voice that kept asking "Am I the crazy one here?"

Ultimately, hearing my colleagues vocalise their own objections so strongly translated into a validation of *me*. Maybe I wasn't crazy after all. I am reminded of what happened after I was raped and the reactions of various people around me in the aftermath. It occurred at a private school for developmentally disabled young adults where I was a teacher and the perpetrator was a student. Certainly there were some sympathetic voices from fellow teachers but some of the more vocal reactions were from the school administration, which essentially placed the blame on me. (I should either have been able to defend myself or I should have known better than to place myself in that situation.) I have always labelled this view as emerging out of self-interest and an inability to accept whatever decisions on their part contributed to the event's circumstances. But I'm also seeing more and more that perhaps they were speaking a truth as they saw it – that is, that women are vulnerable and the violence inflicted on them is just a reality of life, something to be accepted and dealt with – but which ultimately and perhaps conveniently perpetuates its existence. This notion was explicitly expressed when I was raped and implicitly accepted when the Carol Doll was abused. Thus I am sitting with the idea that there is yet another dimension of feminine courage: the collective willingness of women to live a life openly in a world that at its centre does not welcome them, whilst nevertheless sustaining the illusion that we live in a civilised society.

I am tempted to wallow in the paralysis of utter frustration as I consider the enormity of these thoughts, but I am reminded once again of how I've come to know this idea of feminine courage. Much of my doctoral dissertation focused on my journey to find my voice – both literally and figuratively – as I struggled to understand, name and vocalise the experiences of abuse in my life and how forces inside and outside of me kept me silent about their devastating effects. It took courage to validate myself, then more courage to say so out loud. But as one journey ends, another begins and so I am seeing that the courage to find my voice is becoming a foundation to, in turn, give voice to others, and to identify and point to what is unseen and overlooked. A world in which some voices are oppressed to the benefit of others is not one I choose to perpetuate. And I know from first-hand experience that it can be hard for one individual to find a way to speak out, especially if this runs counter to prevailing thought.

With sharper clarity, I know I am speaking out more frequently and hopefully more clearly, but my way forward feels more random and disjointed than purposeful. I get blank looks more often than not when I raise questions not asked before, so I keep pushing back the self-doubt. And when people don't respond by saying, "Of course! Why didn't I see that sooner?" I use my courage to persist anyway.

Just when I'm starting to run out of courage and feel tempted to drop back into the void of silence, I have a moment of what may be validation, that perhaps I am being heard by someone after all. So I have another short story to tell.

Speaking Out and Helping Others to be Heard

I was recently in a meeting with a woman I'll refer to as 'Judith', who works for an organisation I'll call Green Consulting. Green Consulting is a partner in a project that connects to my consulting work and it was suggested that we start to collaborate in the areas where we intersect. While the professional context obligated me to agree to this expansion of my work, it was with some trepidation because of an earlier experience I'd had with the owner of the firm, 'Bob Green'. In simple and direct terms, based on my encounter with him several months earlier, I would describe Bob as a controlling predator.

At the time, I was with a few clients who thought that Bob and Green Consulting would be a good partner for a project that my team was just getting underway. Although the meeting was supposed to be an exploratory discussion, Bob took immediate control of the agenda and insisted that we begin our conversation by using a technique I'll refer to as 'playing back'. This consisted of Bob sharing his view of the business opportunity, in great detail, and then requiring that a designee repeat back everything he said until he was sure you had heard him correctly. This took several painful rounds until Bob deemed the responses 'correct', at which point the people in our group waived our right to have Bob playback our expectations and the meeting moved on. At this point, Bob went into more detail about his view of the project, which included a description of a new job role that I would take on under his direction. What he had in mind didn't fit either my understanding or intentions, so when I was able to jump in I offered up an alternative view. As he listened to me, he steepled his fingers and nodded his head, his lips pursed. Then as I wrapped up my thoughts, he took a breath and spun his swivel chair. As he came full circle he planted his feet, locked eyes with me and declared "I completely disagree!" What ensued was a diatribe detailing how wrong I was and asserting that the project would be a complete and utter failure if we did anything of the sort. He was clearly in attack mode and it was all I could do to find a stance that would keep me from getting sucked in. Our exchange went on for several minutes, with Bob getting more heated by the moment, until the lead client suddenly cut in. "Bob," he said carefully and deliberately. "Could you see me out in the hallway?"

The Bob that returned was much more demure and, once the meeting was over, the group I was with agreed that there wasn't a collaborative fit between our two organisations; but I had this episode lodged in my memory six months later when I was again approached to partner with his firm. After a brief discussion with my client, I agreed to do so only if Bob was not an active participant. So there I was, meeting with Judith and her fellow colleagues as we began a whiteboard session aimed at mutually addressing our clients' business problem.

Since I had been direct and open about my unwillingness to work with their organisation's most senior leader (without repeating all the details of our initial encounter), I wasn't surprised when Judith brought up my objections and came to Bob's defence. She was genuinely concerned that whatever had transpired between us was an anomaly of sorts (although she acknowledged that he could be a bit of a jerk on occasion) and that it was really more a matter of his being misunderstood. She then spent quite a bit of time describing his many good attributes – his personal generosity to her, the causes he gave time and money to, the kindness he expressed to his staff (he'd hosted everyone for drinks on Christmas Eve since he considered them all part of his family) and so on. Not wishing to get into a debate, I simply nodded a lot. (Although as she went on, I'll confess that I had a twinge of self-doubt, the old 'Is it just me?' kind.) Nonetheless, she finally wrapped up her defence of Bob and our work continued.

Soon thereafter, a young new colleague of Judith's, Alex, joined us to help organise our notes. He brought in his laptop and dutifully began transcribing the scribbles we had made all over the walls while Judith and I continued with our meeting. As she and I talked, Judith began to speculate that she might need at least to share with Bob the gist of our ideas, at which point she paused and added, "Although I suppose we should be a bit cautious, because you never know with him."

At this point, Alex looked up from his work, gave a quick nod and said, "I know what you mean. The first time I met him – at my job interview – he called me fat."

I hadn't been paying too much attention to him, but now I quickly looked up and examined him more closely. He was in his early twenties with curly brown hair and pleasant eyes. He was built squarely, much like an American football player, but 'fat' didn't immediately come to mind. Not sure how to respond, I simply said, "Ummm hmmm," and turned to Judith, who had a frown on her face. She leaned closer to Alex. "He did? He said that?" she asked.

Alex kept his head down, intent on copying our notes. "Actually," he said matter-of-factly as he punched away at his keyboard, "he called me fat and undisciplined."

Judith's mouth was now open and she was sputtering. "He really said that!? Why – why that's *illegal!*"

Since I was about to say so myself, I only nodded in agreement and continued "umm hmmm-ing," at which point Alex seemed to realise exactly what he'd just said and who he was saying it about. "Well, actually, um, he had a point," he said, some anxiety now creeping into his voice. "We were at the gym working out and Bob is pretty buff for an old guy, so really, I can see why he'd say that."

Judith continued to sputter about the illegality of the situation, at which point I finally responded by simply saying, "You're right. It is." A few years ago I might have wanted to break the tension and soothe those in the room, but in the moment I was satisfied to simply let the thoughts land.

Telling the story from a few weeks' distance has helped me to see a chain of conversations that I didn't anticipate, nor quite connect until a few days later. In the first links of the chain, I experience something I consider unacceptable, and choose to say so even as I wonder if I'll be heard. Nothing changes until a few chain links later when I see that my voice has now created a shift that supports the voice of another, and together we are now heard. This is some of the reinforcement that I need: that I am not always heard the first (or second or third) time; that something that is hard to say can also be hard to hear; and that by finding my voice I create a space that allows others to share their voice also.

The Opportunity of 'Shaping Voice'

I have reflected on the work I've done in *finding my voice* and then more recently of then using this experience to *give voice* to what I see and feel around me, and in ways that others cannot. That seems like plenty to reflect and focus on but, in talking with my colleagues, they have pointed out that there is a third experience happening: I also have the opportunity to *shape voices* through my consulting.

I think of the word 'shape' as another way of saying 'influence' or 'coax'. And it is in this shaping that I am socially constructing the world I'm a part of with my clients.

To borrow from my doctoral dissertation, in a social constructionist's view of the world, "It is through the daily interactions between people in the course of social life that our versions of knowledge become fabricated." (Burr, 2003: 4). Therefore, we are creating the world through our dialogue and, in doing so, opening up new kinds of conversations and therefore new kinds of conclusions.

'Dialogue' truly is the centre of this third part of my work and what's interesting to me is that, while it is sometimes squarely in the room, it is often most important and powerful in the conversations that are happening along the edges. In fact, I sometimes think about my work as being 'stealth': that is, I bring forward questions, ideas and issues that go well beyond the formal engagement I was contracted for (which is centred on doing skill building for a thousand people who work directly with the customers). Yet I believe that the culture is so closely entwined with the other work I do, to ignore it is at the peril of all of us. So I find myself treading into uncharted territory, essentially taking on a far bigger project, with 'dialogue' as the means to the end.

I 'shape voice' when I talk to the team that is rewriting the corporate values and offer to 'tweak things'. I later see that my tweaks have made the final edits and it's being launched worldwide.

I 'shape voice' when I offer to summarise a meeting on ways to improve the culture and later see my summary used in several other presentations.

I 'shape voice' when I think that what I've said has fallen on deaf ears, only to hear later it's been repeated to others several times over.

I 'shape voice' when my client has me edit critical documents so that the message he is intending is clear and focused. And while I'm doing so, I suggest additional ideas that also make it into the final version.

But there is still much to be done. I have a daughter who is a young adult and just starting off in the working world. She has chosen to pursue a career in technology and she too is a pioneer, finding her voice in an industry that has fewer women in it today than there were twenty years ago. In her first job out of college, she landed with a small high-tech firm and fairly bubbled with enthusiasm as she shared bits about her colleagues, her projects and her aspirations. She brought a lot of energy to her work and wanted to help build an organisation that made products she cared about, but in a way that brought out the best in the entire team. Things were going beautifully, but after a year they assigned her to work for a man who she was wary about. She never explained why, only that they didn't 'see eye to eye'. Nevertheless, she was optimistic and was anxious to learn and contribute.

As time went by, her wariness increased – and then turned to weariness as her energy subsided. Then she must have reached a crossroad of sorts as she commented to me during a recent conversation that it might be time to look for another job. Before she could act on this, though, the decision was made for her: she called last week, clearly distraught, and shared that she'd been let go.

She couldn't quite explain why, and I knew that her performance and work ethic couldn't be the reason. However, a few days later, after she'd had time to clear her head and talk to a few people (including a leader who had left the organisation previously), she shared with me what she felt had happened. "It was the culture, Mom. In the end, I didn't fit in with them."

So here I am, seeing the cycle continue over three decades later as I consider how I, too, was a young woman, full of energy, and was ultimately driven out (and worse) because I also 'didn't fit in'. So I feel an even stronger sense of urgency, I fret at the massive noise in the system and I hope, ultimately, that I can be heard over the din.

CHAPTER 6

A Dialogue about Getting Physical

Jennifer's work provoked us into a rather heated conversation about the hypocrisy, as we see and have experienced it, around 'the body at work'. There appears to be a pretence that we are supremely rational beings and that our bodies are merely incidental, despite the continued prevalence of sexual harassment (McDonald, 2012) and of intimate relationships (Biggs et al., 2012) in the workplace, which would suggest that our bodies most certainly are present at work.

On his way to our meeting, John had spotted an advert on the train for influenza medication that suggested we keep going, even when we're really ill, because we now have the very best symptom suppressants. His mention of the particular potion in turn triggered a conversation about the lowly status our bodies generally have acquired in white Western cultures, which not surprisingly, got us onto Sarah Beart's work.

Kathleen: Sarah's right I think, when she says that we think of our body as an instrument that we have, rather than as an integral part of who we are. It's almost as if our bodies are traitors we are tied to unwittingly. Thus our body language betrays what 'is really going on below the surface' and decisions based on emotions are 'irrational' and not to be trusted (Simon, 1989) in contrast with 'rational decisions' which are considered intentional, reasoned and goal-oriented.

John: Which is ironic, considering we now know the importance emotions play in any decision-making process (Pfister and Böhm, 2008). It appears we can't even make simple economic decisions if the emotional part of our brain is impaired (Koenings and Tranel, 2007), let alone chose a holiday destination, a strategic direction for our company or a life partner!

Kathleen: We humans really are full of contradictions! We like to believe that our perception of [organisational] life is grounded in comprehensive and current research, and yet we find ways to ignore that research, when it's too different from our habitual assumptions. Similarly, we continue to disappear [the significance of] our bodies in the public sphere, whilst the 'body beautiful' has never been more prevalent and obsessed over in the media. I often wonder whether it is the fact that our bodies really do not behave like machines, and continue to be unpredictable, despite our most potent intervention strategies, that leads us to try to ignore them.

John: I am particularly struck by the contrast between the contemporary obsession with the human body, on the one hand, and its utter neglect, in my experience, in an organisational context. So much of our body and bodily functions is considered embarrassing or taboo.

Kathleen: Jennifer and Sarah each break different facets of that taboo. By raising issues of gender, Jennifer refers to people's physical characteristics, however implicitly. Moreover, her research goes into the physical violence perpetrated against her as a young female employee. At the time of writing this book, the extent of sexual harassment is once again shockingly topical.

John: Sarah's research also has a gendered aspect of course, given that intuition and working with one's gut feelings tends to be associated with women and the home, rather than with the supposedly strictly rational territory of organisations. She really does deliver a double whammy. Not only does she challenge the 'leave your body at home' injunction, she insists on paying careful attention to her physical sensations as a valuable source of information for herself and her clients. In my view, that amounts to the equivalent of bursting a whole dam of introjections and norms.

Kathleen: [Laughs] I had quite a visceral experience there of a wall of water coming at me. Sarah would approve I think, me paying attention to my physical response… You are right though. Her research shows how our bodies might tell us valuable information about ourselves and our clients, because, as descendants of herd animals, we are wired to pick up signals about the other at a physical level. This assertion inevitably challenges our habitual view of ourselves as separate and discrete individuals.

John: This seems to me deeply important for anyone engaged in supporting people through change. If change is likely to trigger anxiety in our clients then we are bound to pick that up and carry some of it. Provided I have a well-developed sense of what my physical state is telling me, I have access to information about my client, which I can draw on during our interaction. Also being able to hold anxiety well signals to my client, at an embodied level, that the situation may be scary but is still safe enough.

Kathleen: Being able to keep a level of physical comfort and assurance, however anxiety provoking the situation may be, is reassuring for the other in a way no amount of verbal soothing alone can achieve. Seeing people as connected in this way does run counter to our Western individualist culture though. And it is deeply ingrained. I recall my discomfort when Brian Goodwin, leading a morning meditation at Schumacher College, gently reminded us that the air filling his lungs had, only moments before, travelled through the bodies of each us. I don't know about the others, but I was rather shocked at that idea.

John: I think our individualist, rationalist tradition has deprived us of an important source of comfort: another's physical presence. There seems to be a cut-off point in childhood, beyond which it is no longer acceptable to run for comfort into the arms of another. We're a bit more lenient for women resting on a strong man's shoulder, of course. But only when there's a romantic angle... I know, I'm being cynical, but I do believe we have conflated the joy and learning we can experience in another's physical presence with sexual attraction. In a way, reclaiming the heritage of our physical nature is reclaiming safe ground. There can be something deeply soothing about the physical presence of others, but it means we need to get comfortable with our own bodies and become explicitly interested in what they are telling us in the first place.

CHAPTER 7

Taking My Body to Work – Working with Relational Embodiment in Coaching and Consulting Practice

By Sarah Beart

How do things really happen in organisations? I've been fascinated by this question ever since my very first working experiences. I spent those early days in a mixture of settings: global corporates, venerable public-sector establishments and small entrepreneurial businesses, learning really useful lessons about matters such as how strategy really takes shape, what qualities of relationship it takes for teams to work well under pressure and how to handle requests for a left-handed screwdriver. After abandoning my early intentions to be a materials scientist, I spent some years working as a British diplomat, which gave me fewer opportunities to work with screwdrivers but plenty to get interested in inter-organisational relationships and the importance of language and culture in how things change.

I find myself still with an insatiable curiosity (plain old nosiness perhaps!) about the business of organising. This curiosity keeps me in a line of work that I really enjoy: helping leaders and teams get things working better (or even better) than they currently do. My current fascination is with the question of how to live and organise in "Liquid Times" (as sociologist Zygmunt Bauman calls them). How do we navigate the organisational waters in the face of what can feel like perpetual reorganisation and endemic unpredictability, coupled with ever-increasing demands for certainty and high performance? When I'm at risk of getting too serious about this, my husband and two children will remind me that it's time for a game of 'It'.

Starting with Practice

I am sitting on a slightly scratchy sofa in an anonymous office in a noisy part of central London, drinking tea with a new coaching client. We are just starting to get to know each other, exchanging something of our life stories, our current experience and roles. I know something of the very large organisation she works in, having already worked with one or two other senior executives. My brief from her organisation is to provide coaching support with a consulting flavour to help her lead the very significant changes her new role requires.

As she begins to talk about this job and some of the difficulties she's experiencing she appears to get more and more animated and then even agitated. I am paying attention to what she is saying about her team, her boss and her peers, who they are and what they do, how they all work together, the structures, targets and customers, the pressures and demands of the reorganisation, the cost-cutting and redundancies. There's a lot of information to take in. I take some notes and sketch the structures to check that I understand what she's saying.

While paying close attention to these important 'facts', I am giving just as much attention to different 'facts': information about myself. I am paying attention to my emotional, physical and sensory experience, attending to the way these experiences flow alongside the conversation. For a while it is just that: a somewhat undifferentiated flow. I gradually become aware that my image of her is shifting, as though she is moving in and out of focus for me. I blink and my image of her blurs and wobbles, distorts. I also notice that she appears to be talking to some point on the wall behind me, as though her eyes are focused elsewhere.

I begin to feel what I describe to myself as a nervous sort of buzz in my stomach and a slight sense of disorientation. I am still taking a few notes, while increasingly wondering about my physical sensations. She begins to talk about a lack of confidence in her own performance, about how good her recent 360 appraisal was, the compliments of her boss and yet how she can't quite believe that this is serious. I am wondering about blurry vision, musing on the idea that I am finding it hard to see her and she may not be seeing me. I have no idea what any of this might mean for us, but I say in response to her lack of belief in the 360 "It's almost as though you don't see yourself at work."

The conversation takes a sudden turn, from my point of view at least. Suddenly she is in sharp focus for me, staring straight at me. She agrees, then quite abruptly begins to tell me an apparently unrelated story about a time in her life when she was quite deliberately ostracised from her social circle. The topic of being seen comes to the fore as it slowly emerges that, back then, being seen held dangers for her. We talk about this at some length. She speaks simply about the effects on her confidence, how risky it can feel to be seen and be successful and the penalties she imagines for being unsuccessful. She says she's surprised to find herself telling me this – it's not something she has talked to many people about. We get into some further conversation, and begin to think about some practical matters relating to her team and the reorganisation. Towards the end of our time together, she asks how I am seeing her. I take a moment to look again, carefully and deliberately, and describe to her both what I have seen and heard in the course of our conversation.

The Background to My Inquiry – How ADOC Worked for Me

I am starting with a description of my practice to give a feel for the way I work these days. It's different from the way I worked before embarking on ADOC. Back then, I would have had as good, or perhaps better, grasp of all the conventional data, the organisation charts and spreadsheets. If I had even noticed my physical experience as we'd talked I would have ignored, dismissed or tried to suppress it – probably wondering what was wrong with my contact lenses or thinking that I needed to say something really intelligent to catch my client's attention so she'd look at me. These days my practice is different. I have come (slowly) to re-include and value the full range of my physical, emotional, intellectual and imaginal experiences as I work. I start from the premise that they have something useful about them for the work I'm doing, even if I'm not immediately sure what that is.

Taking my experience seriously has at times felt like an extreme sport – risky, unpredictable and not for the fainthearted. At the start I was reluctant to admit I even had a body, still less that I took it to work. As I gradually began to notice how I'd been living, I wrote that I:

> had been behaving as if it were just some kind of shopping trolley that I used to cart my head around. I did my best to take care of this vehicle. I fuelled it, cleaned it and maintained it, although the effects of gestating two babies in it seemed to have bent it out of shape quite badly.

This metaphor made people laugh, many with a kind of wry recognition.

At the same time, I was noticing just how much of my consulting work also had a metaphorical quality – strange images and ideas would often come to mind as I worked. Sometimes I would share them, with close colleagues and friends, but with clients I usually kept them to myself. What, after all, could they have to say that could be of any value in comparison to my thinking – my thinking after all was what had been applauded all my life. I had a ready answer to a colleague's question "why do bright girls deny their bodies?" Because their minds are much more acceptable.

In a moment I want to say more about just how and why bodies, and especially women's bodies, have come to be so problematic in modern organisations. But now I want to say a little about the process of ADOC. This business of 'taking my body to work' was not at all where I started. Instead I was fired up by an intuitive determination to do a doctorate and to work on the idea of parallel process, the way in which consultants or consulting teams can come to experience the relational patterns of their clients.

This was born out of a real-life experience of my own during my MBA studies, consulting to a very large engineering business with a brief to improve strategic buyer–supplier relationships. After an incident in which a colleague and I had felt badly treated by our client, I began to notice we seemed to be experiencing the same feelings we'd noticed in the suppliers, and were feeling tempted into the kind of supplier behaviour which our organisational clients complained bitterly about. We began to think we were developing a living understanding of how these very important relationships went wrong and to understand how both parties were experiencing the other. But we couldn't find a way to talk about this insight and were worried about upsetting our clients. Later I joined Ashridge Consulting and encountered the term 'parallel process' as a way to describe this kind of experience, and thought I would read up on what to do about it. Discovering that not much was written, I began to develop a good deal of energy for researching this through ADOC and decided to explore the MBA experience again. The following is part of my exploration into that parallel process:

> One dark and chilly morning at 6 a.m., a colleague and I completed a long journey to a manufacturing plant where an important supplier meeting was to take place, one we were due to observe. Our client showed up about an hour late and breezily explained that he and "management" had changed their mind "a few days ago" and we would no longer be allowed to attend. We were furious, too furious to speak. On the way home we began by speculating and conspiracy theorising: what was going on in the meeting that meant we couldn't be allowed to attend? Why had no-one bothered to tell us before our 4 a.m. start? Gradually our attention turned to plotting: how to meet our contractual requirements without needing our client's cooperation.

> Suddenly we had an insight: we were having an authentic supplier experience. The suppliers had hinted to us that they often felt at the mercy of their customer's whims, that they felt badly treated as people, that they were often shut out of important decisions that would affect what they were being asked to provide. And they acknowledged that sometimes they behaved badly in return, often without the customer really noticing or appearing to care. We got even more excited as we began to see that we were responding to our experience in much the same way as the suppliers. Feeling angry and poorly treated, we had spent time bad-mouthing the organisation and its people.

> Then we decided to keep our mouths shut about how we felt and concentrate on getting the research material we needed out of the relationship without much regard for the consulting project. Our supervisor had told us at the start that if things got difficult, we were to remember that he was our real customer. We found ourselves surprised to notice how little we now cared to do a good consulting job for our organisation client.

> This insight felt exciting, precious and dangerous. We debated for weeks whether to "say something" to our client and about the likely consequences. We wanted to offer a view of how the organisation might appear to its suppliers, some possible explanations of how the relationships went wrong and some ideas about how they might change.

> But it felt difficult to find ways of raising these issues without seeming critical of our friendly client. We didn't want to wound him personally. Nor did we want to get kicked out as consultants, because we had a dissertation to write. We worried that our feelings and experiences wouldn't be taken seriously in this very traditional engineering organisation and so we kept quiet, dutifully completing our contracted piece of work. In truth, we played our supplier role perfectly – and to this day I regret it.

I embarked on ADOC resolved to find ways to use these parallel-process experiences in the interests of my clients. I told myself that I would pay more attention to my own experiences, at the time of course little knowing what I'd been ignoring

An Unlikely Beginning?

My being fired up to take on a doctorate was perhaps surprising. When the doctorate was launched and applications invited, I was on maternity leave following the birth of my second child and preparing to return to work part time at Ashridge: not perhaps the obvious time to begin a demanding programme of study. Amidst the concerns of friends and family, and in defiance of all rational argument, I was absolutely determined to begin. I later came to realise that the experiences of pregnancy and childbirth had confronted me with my own long-ignored embodiment and thus opened up the possibility of working in the territory of the body. In the end, I think I did my doctoral work because of my children rather than (as might be more conventionally asserted by working mothers) despite them. This entanglement of life and practice was not necessarily something I'd expected at the start, but looking back I think it is probably a necessary aspect of an action-inquiry process. As Rosemarie Anderson suggests (Anderson, 2006), researchers can often find themselves researching something that they have been carefully avoiding or ignoring for much of their life.

I began the work with huge enthusiasm and determination, reading everything I could lay my hands on about the topic of parallel process from the worlds of social work and psychotherapy, and comfortably passed the first major written hurdle. Then it all started to go wrong. I completely lost interest in my own topic and felt utterly bored as I went through the motions of talking with other consultants about it (they still seemed pretty interested though). All my good rational methods were failing. I'd committed to myself to being thoroughly interested in the phenomena of my inquiry and taking my own experience seriously, so I uncomfortably thought I'd better take the extremely inconvenient and unwelcome phenomenon of my loss of interest seriously too, even though I thought I had no idea where this would take me.

Some aspect of me did have ideas though; I started to have quite extraordinary and disturbing dreams. At a loss for what else to do and at the prompting of my supervisor Robin Ladkin, I began to work actively with these dreams as part of my inquiry process. Lots of the dreams involved what I would now see as archetypal and alchemical imagery – dragons, roses, silver ladies, sick men, sulphurous prisons and dungeons, murderers and witches, palaces and weddings. Working with this kind of material was not comfortable for my established rational, intellectual, mind-over-matter perspective. It seemed as though the universe was generously cooperating at this time, by arranging for most of my consulting work to be cancelled. I had plenty of time for this particular kind of inquiry as well as for paying rather closer attention than usual to the small amount of consulting work that remained.

Of course, this is the sense I make of it now, with the happy benefit of hindsight and a completed doctorate under my belt. At the time I felt in despair, lost about my topic and in my practice. It was only with the dedicated support and serious challenges of my supervisor and supervision group that I managed to stick with it. I had always been very clear that I didn't want to do a doctorate of the sort that involved a kind of contracted-out bit of research which was part of a grander project for an eminent professor: I wanted to do something that started with me, my practice and my interests. I was also very clear that I wanted some kind of group of people to be working with – that I would need people to talk and think with if I was going to be really creative. As the first ADOC handbook said, the programme was designed to be different from the conventional "solus (and soulless) experiences associated with most other doctorates".

Through this difficult phase my supervision group was astonishingly important: inquiring gently but seriously into the very first of the dreams which I hesitantly related (Robin as tutor and Margaret especially); pressing me to trust this as work (Jill's inquiry into trust linking with mine here); and offering themselves as co-inquirers as my practice began to take shape, with Steve coming and conducting a co-inquiry into what it was like to be my coaching client as I allowed myself to practice in my fully embodied way. At one point, a colleague wondered how I was coping with the combination of consulting workload, small children and the doctorate on top of it all. My honest reply was that the doctorate was in fact support rather than additional burden – the only thing that was keeping me going.

As I think back now, I want to pay some attention to what it was we were doing that was so significant. As a group, we were quite dedicated to writing for each meeting of the supervision group and to reading each other's writing, giving it serious attention before we met. We worked in a kind of action-learning style in supervision group meetings and, through these multiple processes, eventually all of the others' inquiries began to influence and support mine. I remember being held firmly to exercising curiosity about the tiny, taken-for-granted details of my practice by Kevin's emphasis on William Blake's "minute particulars" (Blake, 1804/1951) and taking my strange perceptions seriously with the help of a reminder of Blake's ideas about the "doors of perception" (Blake's *The Marriage of Heaven and Hell*, in Erdman, 1965).

Both in the process of my inquiry and in its content, I am clear that I couldn't have done this without Robin, Jill, Kevin and Steve. Some of this is perhaps obvious and what one might expect from a doctoral group, in that I was learning new ideas and theories from reading their writing and through our conversations. Yet in the relationships between us much more was happening. As I slowly began to value and trust the images and sensations that I was experiencing in my practice, I began to try them out more explicitly with my colleagues, both in the wider ADOC group and in supervision sessions. At one meeting, I saw Jill as Celtic Queen while feeling the tightness of what I imagined to be a coronet against my head; and at another I had a vague sense of Steve as the archetypal Green Man who emerges from the woods at times of crisis. I came to see that these strange experiences of mine were in some way useful to the members of my group, if I could notice and then voice them – this gave me confidence in my emerging practice and encouragement to work more seriously with clients in these somewhat unusual ways.

Alchemy as a Method of Inquiry

Looking back at the difficult times, I really don't want to glamorise or glorify this suffering element of the process – it's too tempting to rationalise it as some kind of necessary part of a somewhat heroic journey which I always knew I would complete. I see it now as part of what I came to describe as a Jungian alchemical method, a process in which change and transformation happen through engagement with matter and with intellect, and through entering what Jung called the *nigredo*, the dark depths of distress and despair (Jung, 1953, 1967). For me, this is not a once-in-a-lifetime business – it wasn't for Jung either. Rather it is a cyclical process of development and learning which I can expect to re-enter and work with for the rest of my life. Right now I'm in another phase of extraordinary dreaming, dreams full of symbols and images, of castles, furnace fires and raging floods; so I know that there is some further work required of me, of which this writing is probably part.

This was another exciting and demanding aspect of ADOC – the requirement to develop one's own methods of inquiry. My alchemical methods required me to draw together my former (and long-ago abandoned) love of chemistry and my passion for psychology, and to create a method for my doctorate that would allow me to embark on work that I needed to do but could not yet really describe. The alchemy of the ancients required the alchemists to work with matter (in the laboratory) and with the spiritual and intellectual (praying and reading in the library), and this turned out to be an excellent discipline for my own work (e.g. Jung, 1953, 1967; Edinger, 1985). For a long while I took alchemy as a somewhat abstract metaphor for my work – and it was really rather late (almost embarrassingly late!) that I took seriously the requirement for working with matter – and suddenly saw that the 'matter' I had been working with was quite literally the physical matter of my own body. Alchemists were assumed to need to go through periods of darkness and suffering if they were to be worthy of the work, to find the metaphorical or literal 'gold' at the end of the process; and so I came to understand that for my alchemical inquiry the difficult times were a necessity.

The Minute Particulars of Practice

With the encouragement of my supervision group, I began to pay attention to the minutiae of my work with clients, particularly coaching clients. This part of the process was not about developing something brand new by learning from outside myself, but rather developing and amplifying aspects of my practice that were latent and undervalued. I thought everyone experienced a steady flow of images, ideas, metaphors and associations as they listened to what their clients said. Sometimes I used these actively and clients seemed to find them both surprising and useful. The following vignette from my doctorate speaks to my emerging internal attention and practice and its potential for practical value to clients.

> I remember a coaching conversation of many years ago with an actuarial partner who was worried about his time management… He felt he ought to deal with things that arrived in his various in-trays immediately, but found himself just leaving them. As we talked, it became apparent that he was struggling with a tension.

He knew that he worked best when he could leave some of them aside, to think about both consciously and unconsciously, while others needed to be dealt with immediately. But having read the latest time-management books, he still believed that he ought to prioritise things and then deal with everything pretty well straight away in order of importance.

I found myself starting to think about food (perhaps it was close to lunchtime) and proposed to him that the papers and emails that arrived could be viewed as cheeses. Some of them would go off if not consumed immediately and be at best unpleasant and at worst injurious to health if left. Others were unpalatable until they had been given a chance to mature in a cool dark place, perhaps like good Cheddar and Parmesan. He laughed a lot at this seemingly wild idea. And something changed in his view of how he might act that I don't think could have changed with logical arguing about 'oughts' and 'shoulds', about correct time management and prioritisation. He suddenly felt he could allow himself time to think and that, actually, cheese identification was both more useful and more amusing as a stance to take towards his in-box. He could, as I now see it, allow himself his own knowing about how he worked most effectively.

More often than not I was just vaguely aware of my flow of images and carried on with my conscious listening or conversation. Gradually, I began to notice just how much there was in the flow, how much of it was physical or sensory as well as in the form of images and associations, and how useful it seemed to be if I found ways of using it with my clients and in supervision. Didn't everyone experience this? No, came the resounding answer from my group – or at least not nearly as much as you. As I began to pay more attention, I tuned in to physical experiences of cold and heat, strange sensations of discomfort, terror or excitement, loops of film running in my mind, snatches of music or images from fairy tales. I had been an obsessive reader of stories and Greek mythology as a child, and noticed how often I found myself drawing on what my doctoral friends have described as "a rich treasure trove of images and ideas", many of them with links to Jungian archetypes (Jung, 1959).

I used these ways of working not just in my encounters with clients, but also to support me in developing myself in my doctoral work. Using on oneself the same methods that one proposes to use with others, and to do this "with the same relentlessness, consistency and perseverance" (Jung, 1954: 73), is good Jungian and Action Research practice. I worked actively with my dreams, painted pictures (distinctly reluctantly at the start) and worked with the metaphors that arose. In conversation with my supervision group, I uncovered a provocative and sustaining analogy in Philip Pullman's *Subtle Knife* (1997), which evoked for me the sense of having a sharp and powerful gift that could cut holes between worlds, one that needed to be used with care and integrity.

The silver unicorn that begins this chapter emerged in painting, following contemplation of the unicorn as an archetypal symbol of the union of the masculine and the feminine (Jung, 1953). Medieval alchemists (who were usually men) often worked with a feminine assistant described as the *soror mystica* or mystical sister. I had found myself first curious and then furious about the way that neither alchemical writings nor Jung himself gave much attention to the role of these women, and wondered about my own practice as *soror mystica* in relation to my alchemical male clients. These methods felt both stretching and supportive. I'd been overtly working in the realm of the intellectual and the emotional, but daring to extend my explicit knowing into the realms of dreams and the body took (literally and metaphorically) heart and nerve: both of which my group and my supervisor helped me to find.

I also took my inquiry out to other practitioners. At the conference held to celebrate the tenth anniversary of the AMOC programme, I held a breakout session which I called 'Embodied Intuition in Consulting Practice', inviting people to join me in answering the following:

When you are working with clients, as a coach or consultant, do you ever:

- *Find that images, film characters, books, works of art or pieces of music come to mind?*

- *Notice and pick up on the metaphors that you and your clients are using?*

- *Become aware of bodily sensations that you attribute to the work you are doing?*

If you answered 'yes' to any of these questions, what do you do with, or about, what you are experiencing?

I had the usual conference nerves – will anyone come to my session? If they do, will I find what they say helpful? Fear flowed through me – fear that people would tell me my territory was already thoroughly explored and mapped, fear at the possibility that what I was saying would have absolutely no resonance or interest for fellow practitioners. I held my breath (and catch myself holding it again now as I write). Firstly a trickle, then more and then the room was full to bursting, crammed with people like me who could answer 'yes' to the first three questions and didn't know how to respond to the fourth. I began to realise that my inquiry was about developing my own responses to this question and that I was going to need some further help. I described this phase, and the new fear that accompanied it, as being like having a tiger by the tail. I felt I didn't know properly what I was doing, that I had no solid theoretical territory to occupy and that I was going to be solely responsible for working it all out not just for myself but to help others too. Of course, now I see that I was thoroughly in the territory of good Action Research which is "for me, for us, for them" (Reason and Marshall, 1987).

Then, with the kind of serendipity that was such a feature of my inquiry, my Pilates teacher (who knew something of my interests) told me about her work with a local body–mind teacher and therapist, Kama Korytowska, and suggested I try out one of her classes. I went, telling my supervision group how nervous I was about embarking on the work because the recommended teacher "doesn't really do words". "Good", they chorused, "sounds just what you need".

I began to work with Kama Korytowska, as a kind of supervisor/therapist for the work that I was doing, both in ADOC and with my client work. Kama introduced me to a whole new body (!) of theory (e.g. Aposhyan, 2004; Bainbridge Cohen, 1994; Hartley, 2009). As Susan Aposhyan puts it in her introduction to Bainbridge Cohen's work, "Not only can we be aware *of* each part of our physical self, we can be aware *with* each part of our physical self." This includes the skeleton, ligaments, muscles, fascia (the thin sheets of tissue between our muscles), fat, skin, endocrine glands, nerves, fluids, breath. I began to learn to be aware both *of* and *with* my physical self, understanding my own body history so that I could be aware of what I brought to each encounter with clients, as well as what they brought themselves. For example, with one new client I had experienced a nearly paralysing feeling of disgust as we talked. Some of the work that I did with Kama was to sense my way into this disgust, disentangling what part of this disgust was mine about myself (about my relationship to my own fat), and how much of it might be said to belong usefully and appropriately to my relationship with the client and his relationships within his own organisation. It was useful to begin to develop a discipline, a kind of bodily reflective practice using all kinds of methods.

One aspect of our work together that was both surprising and revealing was learning how to pay attention to the qualities of experience, and to do this without trying to change the experience. So, for example, feeling stiffness somewhere as I worked, I might instinctively try to stretch, to relieve it. Kama required me to stay with the sensations and be curious, to wonder about them and notice how they changed as I paid attention. To locate them and feel their qualities – sensations of thickness or solidity, of flow or of density, chills in the blood or ramrods in my back. And then to inquire into and with these sensations, rather than trying to force change on them.

Kama also invited me to become aware of my urges to movement and to work with action. As she pointed out, we attempt to do so much of the work of paying attention to ourselves in absolute stillness. Today, if I ask practitioners on the Ashridge Masters in Change to pay attention to how they are in their bodies, they will typically sit stock still. And yet our bodies are in continuous flow, change and movement. If we are attentive to ourselves, we can often catch urges to move, which we may or may not choose to act on. These urges to movement sometimes arise simultaneously with images – so for example, when the image of a Celtic Queen first arose in connection with Jill's work, I had a simultaneous sensation of a tight band around my forehead, as though wearing a particularly tight-fitting tiara or crown, and the felt urge to rub my head to relieve the discomfort – a move perhaps to take off the crown? (If you have read Jill's earlier chapter, you'll find out more about this and what happened to the Celtic Queen!)

Why is "Do You Take Your Body to Work?" Such an Extraordinary Question in Twenty-first-century Northern Europe? – A Wildly Exciting Theory

Through my work with Kama, I began to engage much more seriously with my own embodiment, and to get deeply interested in why and how this seemed such a fraught subject, not just for me but for others too. This was a topic that came up in my conversations with John Higgins as we began developing this chapter. "Why," he wondered, "was I so wary of writing about my work, and just why was the bodily such a problem in organisations?" In response, I shared with him some of the historical context as I understand it – and I got such a 'now I get it!' response that I thought I'd better say something about this here.

It's been rather fashionable in organisational circles to blame Descartes for the privileging of rational thinking, planning and of intellectual approaches to the field of organisations, management, leadership and consulting. And of course, his idea that there is a thinking bit of us (*res cogitans*) separate from our physical selves (*res extensa*) has played its part. But I think discomfort with the bodily (at least for North Americans and Northern Europeans) has been increasing steadily for centuries, and some of the reading that I did in the course of ADOC showed me just how far back it goes.

My first encounter with the historical context was in reading the work of Norbert Elias (Elias, 1994). If anyone had suggested to me at the start of ADOC that I would experience wild physical excitement – get hot, have a racing pulse – while reading the translated master work of a dead German sociologist, I would have bet good money against it. But Elias's work *The Civilizing Process* got me hooked as I read about how societies have used shame as a method of social control, and how deliberately creating rules and sanctions about bodily matters has pushed the body and bodily drives back behind a steadily advancing shame frontier. Incidentally, it took me a good while to begin to use and trust my *physical* responses to theory – the dullness and sense of the world closing in as I read some authors and the sense of life, light, turbulence, agitation or sheer excitement as I read others. I had a similar burst of wild excitement reading Lakoff and Johnson's *Philosophy in the Flesh* (1999), struggling desperately to convey to my supervision group what they were saying and why this was a world-changing work. I couldn't explain to my own or to their satisfaction, but they trusted that for me this mattered and pressed me to pursue it.

Management, Organisations and the Body

In the early part of the twentieth century, William Frederick Taylor began to develop and promote his ideas about the organisation of work. Taylor is arguably the founder of the professions of management and management consulting, paving the way for the many professions that change and consulting practitioners work in today, such as human resources and organisation development. It's pretty well known that Taylor made a great deal of systematising the way organisations were run; but what has been called to attention rather more recently is his attitude to bodies (Bahnisch, 2000).

Taylor himself was a pretty small and wiry man and he longed, by all accounts, to be a "muscular six footer" who could take on the factory workers (Bahnisch, 2000). Perhaps because of his own physical limitations, he began to get interested in the separation of physical and thinking work. He watched what the men did in the Bethlehem Steel Foundry and reckoned that he could get men who were shifting around 12.5 tons of steel a day to shift about three times that – and if he was smart, he could get them to do it by paying only about 30 to 60 per cent more. The deal he proposed for what he called a "high-price man" was that the man had to do what he was told – work when he was told to by a manager and rest when he was similarly instructed. In other words, the manager would think with his mind and the worker would use his body. Taylor said in a 1907 lecture "we do not want any initiative in our men" (Taylor, 1907/2008). So you could say that Taylor was operationalising the Cartesian split between mind and body, locating the mind in the manager and the body with the worker.

Tempting as it might be, it would be unfair to blame Taylor or even Descartes for this split because, from a broader perspective, this was merely a perfectly natural next step in a view of bodies that had been unfolding for several thousand years. Elias offers a fascinating window into the last thousand or so, especially where he writes about the way that etiquette, and in particular the regulation of bodily functions and drives, has been used by the wealthy and aristocratic classes to create and maintain a distance from the middle classes, and the middle classes then to distance themselves from the lower (Elias, 1994).

For example, there is the matter of table manners. As a mother of two children, I notice I am pretty interested in how they behave at the table – and yet reading Elias I was forced to recognise the rather arbitrary nature of the rules that I apply. We all used to eat from the communal dish, either by lifting it to our lips for soup or by taking a lump of whatever was on offer by hand. In the thirteenth century, it was proscribed to drink from this communal dish (Elias, 1994: 73). Spoons came in and, at first, a common spoon was passed around. Then we learned to put food on our own plates with a communal spoon; then a special serving spoon was used, which was not to be licked. This was long before ideas about contagion were developed: the rules arose not from disease prevention but from a desire to exert control through social structures or 'figurations', as Elias would say. Forks came much later. Around the eleventh century, a Greek princess who used a fork to eat was regarded as excruciatingly affected, leading to calls for divine wrath to fall on her. Forks were contentious for centuries and as late as the nineteenth century the British navy is said to have worried that the use of forks was prejudicial to discipline and manliness (Tannahill, 1988).

So far so good, but there were other rules of the table. Around the thirteenth century, it began to be seen as ill-bred to blow your nose on the tablecloth and indecent to pick your nose while eating. Then there was a prohibition on using the same hand to blow your nose as to take meat from the communal dish, then one on blowing your nose on your sleeve; and this went on to include not looking in your handkerchief after blowing. By the fifteenth century, good manners included spitting under the table rather than on to it and not touching your body under your clothes with your bare hands at the table.

Bodily functions were also addressed in various guides of the times. The Dutch scholar Erasmus suggested in 1530 that it was impolite to greet someone who was urinating or defecating in the street (where everyone did it). Rather one should pretend that the person engaged in bodily functions did not really exist. By 1570 one should not urinate in front of ladies and, by 1589, one was not supposed to do this on the stairs or in the corridors of the house in which one was a guest (Elias, 1994).

Typically, people in medieval Europe used to share beds – and there were rules about in what order to enter the bed, with the unmarried daughter first in against the wall, furthest from guests. When sharing a bed with a stranger at an inn, it was polite to give one's social superior the first choice of which side to sleep. If one's companion soiled the sheets in the night in 1558, it was impolite to point it out or to invite them to smell it (Elias, 1994: 111).

Ordinary bodily functions that today are unmentionable in polite society (Elias shows how Erasmus had clear and practical advice about farting) gradually came to be relegated to the private sphere, forced behind a steadily advancing shame frontier. Bodies came to have to be segregated from one another in polite society and Elias is clear that this meant that people came to be in very different kinds of relationship with one another – not just at the rational level but also in terms of their emotional connections.

This set me wondering how and why medieval Europeans had come to be developing an increasing sense of shame in relation to their bodies. Going back further still, at least two writers of the Christian New Testament signpost flesh as troublesome and treacherous. St Paul writes to the Philippians (Philippians 3:3, King James Bible) about having "no confidence in the flesh" and muses on the subject of "vile bodies". St Matthew (Matthew 18:8, King James Bible) entertains the possibility that your limbs – your hands or feet – might cause you to stumble or to sin, and advises amputation of the offending part. The spirit, he suggests, may be willing but the flesh is separate, weak and untrustworthy.

And yet even this is not far back enough because a bit more probing takes us to Plato and Aristotle. In Plato's time the body began to be seen as a tomb or prison for the faculty of reason (Grosz, 1994). Continuing with these ideas, Aristotle's biological studies led him to the belief that the role of the male animal was to provide the soul of the offspring and to give form to the "passive shapeless matter" provided by the female (ibid.) At what Grosz calls the threshold of Western reason (ibid.: 5), superior soul and reason are divided from inferior matter and flesh and, in a further twist, the former is allocated to men and the latter to women.

Fast-forwarding to the time of Mary Wollstonecraft's *A Vindication of the Rights of Woman*, it seems that these notions of women had grown in strength (Wollstonecraft, 1792/2004). Wollstonecraft wrote of her concern about the way that women were deforming their bodies in order to adhere to common notions of femininity – professing themselves too weak to take exercise, needing little food and being intellectually incapable. Rousseau had written of the need for women to please men and develop personal charms, whereas men, he argued, needed corporeal powers. I wondered if this was so that they could turn themselves into fodder for Taylor's experiments in steel making.

I think this offers a window into the question of how modern Westerners – and how I – have come to hold a somewhat tricky relationship to our own embodiment. Our bodies are separate from us; they are 'it' rather than 'me'. We think of bodies and perfect bodies as objects we can get – by paying for surgery or cosmetic treatments, by exercising our will at the gym. Bodies are strictly regulated. There is intriguing research about women's bodies that evokes Aristotle: women mustn't leak too much if they want to be taken seriously, so they mustn't cry. They must look fit but not fat, soft but not too sexual, and to be successful must have body sizes and shapes within certain parameters. Both men and women help police these rules (Trethewey, 1999).

It's not easy for men either. As representatives of perfect Platonic ideas they have to be solid, defined, dry. They must show as little flesh as possible – no hairy leg sticking out between the sock and the leg, nothing above the wrist or below the collar, and whatever is underneath the clothing must be firm, never wobbly. Though they have more licence when it comes to body dimensions, they are in the tricky situation of having to show minimum evidence of fluids (look at the fuss when one British Prime Minister was filmed with sweat-stained armpits during a particularly trying party conference). Yet they must also find ways to display their potency – in the form of ties according to one researcher (Harding, 2002). And the computer industry is happy to consider hardware and software, but may use the dismissive term 'wetware' to describe the fallible humans who use their products (more indications that fluids are unwelcome and disorderly).

As we are slowly starting to be able to investigate the brain more closely, I think the mind–body split is being mapped on to the brain–body. There is a huge fascination about what goes on with neuroscience – as long as it's above the neck. The dominant metaphor is an engineering one – the extraordinary machine of the mind controls the far inferior body. The metaphors are revealing: professionals hope to be 'head-hunted' rather than treated as 'hired hands' or mere 'foot-soldiers', showing clearly the status of the head/brain in relation to the rest of the body. And yet we know that our hearts start beating and our guts work long before we have anything we can label a brain and that we have around 500 million neurons in what's now being called the enteric nervous system (Young, 2012).

Implications for Us as Practitioners

The implications of this are serious. We have forgotten that we relate to each other at a bodily level, not just an intellectual one, and that we know with our bodies and through our bodies. The language we use (which we traditionally think of as having nothing to do with our bodies except in relation to those parts of us that make the sound waves of speech) creates sensations and motor responses in ourselves and in others. I am proposing that if we attend to those sensations we can gain a richer and enhanced appreciation of the situations we find ourselves in. We might take seriously Aposhyan's idea that we can sense into each organ of our body, and sense *with* each organ or limb (Bainbridge Cohen, 1994).

In a coaching phone call, a client tells me in calm tones about the acute difficulty he is in regarding a reorganisation. I catch myself developing a startlingly tense and painful sensation in my neck as he speaks, which I relate to him, wondering if it has anything to do with what is happening. He finds this 'spooky' and wonders how I could be feeling the precise kind of pain that he is suffering from, pain which caused him to visit his osteopath the previous day. In my view, this is not spooky – this is an ordinary part of human relating which we (in the West) have been educated out of noticing, let alone acting on.

My excitement on reading Lakoff and Johnson (1999) was in part about their extraordinarily bold and clear linking of the world of metaphor, language and the body. They have three crucial propositions:

- That the mind is inherently embodied
- That thought is mostly unconscious (conservatively, about 95 per cent)
- That abstract concepts are largely metaphorical.

The first assertion is of course a serious challenge to Cartesian thinking – and to all our casual language and thinking that we somehow have a mind outside our physical selves. The second demands that we reconsider the unconscious not as some nasty dark repository for our most reprehensible emotions and desires but as a vast array of vital and valuable processes for keeping us alive, for making sense of the world around us, for detecting subtle cues and dealing with significant threats. Their last proposition argues that all conceptual thinking is metaphorical, that we build a language based on our sensory and motor experiences from gestation onwards, and this makes sense to us because of our shared biology and primary experiences. We describe good relationships as 'close' or 'warm' – because as babies good relationships involve being held close to another and experiencing physical heat. Things that are important are big – because of the importance to us of comparatively large adults when we are small.

There is a constant interplay between our physical experience and our language. I am arguing that as practitioners we often pay attention to the apparent surface logic of language, but are insufficiently attentive to the metaphors our clients and colleagues use. We tend to regard metaphors as too abstract to be any use, mere comparisons or foolish poetry. Yet they can describe experience with exquisite accuracy as well as act as a stimulus to action. One client, stuck in a role far below his capabilities, worked with my image of 'jack-in-the-box', returning to it spontaneously over several meetings as he looked at how he and others kept the lid on the box firmly closed down.

We tend to value our bodily experiences even less than our metaphors – we think there is something wrong with us if strange physical sensations come to our attention in the course of our work. If we feel sick at the prospect of going to see a client we find a bit scary, we may chide ourselves for weakness or unprofessionalism, or regret last night's seafood pizza. I'm arguing we should take this seriously. We can wonder about the pizza for sure, while also being more broadly attentive and curious. Do we always feel sick at the prospect of meeting this person? How does the nausea ebb and flow as we enter her office and discuss our shared business?

This isn't easy of course, not least because in much of the mainstream psychotherapy literature having, and owning up to, these kinds of physical reactions is a sign of trouble in a client and failure in the helper. Only the most troublesome or traumatised clients 'somatise' rather than speak. Even in the body psychotherapy world, many of the practitioners emphasise working *on* others' bodies rather than *with* their own bodies, in mutually embodied relationship. Valuing and working with our own embodied responses in relationship requires vulnerability and discipline. I need to know where the disgust belongs and how to work with it in the interests of my client. In the ordinary world of organisations, we have ceased to notice the ordinariness of our embodied relationships and we have tended to see explicitly physical relationships as falling into one of three categories – parent–child, medical/healing or sexual (Totton, 2002). Being explicit about physical sensations and experiences without care can easily get misinterpreted as taking up a role as parent, doctor or lover: care is needed. With that in mind, I've developed my own short practice guide which is set out below.

Practice Guide for Myself, January 2010

1. **Make contracts** with clients to work in this way, being clear about working with my whole self, about valuing my bodily sensations, my images and metaphors, my feelings as well as my thoughts. Invite my clients to do likewise.

2. **Waiting and attending**. The quality of my practice improves with waiting, with attending with all of my senses and organs. Sooner or later, something of interest will arise; I will become able to answer the questions of where I am alive in my body, what is on my mind, what urges to movement I have. The answers to these questions may not seem convenient, may not make sense to me; let them be.

3. **Registering**. Register what I experience as I work, noting what I experience in connection with particular words being spoken or acts being undertaken. Decouple registering from judgement where you can, be aware of judgements arising. Attend to the strength of the experience, the location of it, its qualities, without trying to change these aspects. Of particular interest are those experiences that seem to carry a charge: the 'subtle knife' moments.

4. **Assume usefulness**. Assume that what arises may be useful and appropriate with the contract that you have. Trust yourself.

5. **Mutuality and intersubjectivity**. I am much more than a passive receiver of information. What I attend to shapes my physiological state and in turn my physiological responses shape those of my colleagues and clients. I assume that, through processes that are not yet well understood, at the liminal edge of consciousness, humans (and of course not just humans) are affected by each other's physiology in multiple ways that are well outside the capabilities of conscious thought.

6. **Hermeneutic**. No seeking after objective truth, some independently verifiable and professional view of 'what is going on here'. Register, and offer something based on what has been registered; try not to interpret for the client. The closer to the original experience the better: if the image comes first, work with that; if the sensation, choose that. If I feel sick, I say that I feel sick; not that what you are saying is about fear or to do with your childhood. Make sense of experiences together: treat the image or sensation as a temporary statement or holding structure, which is open for further interpretation or sense making at any time.

7. **Be specific** with your own experiences and encourage clients to do the same with their own images and sensations. What sort of a dog, exactly? Your stomach, or your small intestine, or your colon? Windpipe or oesophagus? Let go of sensations or images that seem to have no meaning or interest for your client at the moment; get interested if they return.

8. **Play, nicely,** with what you have. Examine images in detail, notice how the sensations change (or don't) as you talk or other matters come into the conversation. Explore the metaphor: if she is the princess, who is the Queen? What story is this? Is there a prince, or a fairy godmother, or other princesses? Who else is in this picture or film? What does the client make of this?

9. **Assume repeating patterns**: be curious about these sensations and images and where else they arise. Where else is there repulsion in the organisation? Who else feels this fear, or urge to run away, or shout for joy? Where else in your own life and your clients' lives?

10. **Get supervision that abides by the Jungian principle** of applying to yourself the same methods that you propose to use with others, and to do so *"with the same relentlessness, consistency and perseverance"* (Jung, 1954: 73). Use supervision in the same way: attending, registering, playing, interpreting, noticing what shifts and how. Go on with supervision and go to supervision routinely, even when you don't feel you need it. Take to supervision those matters that have a charge and yet are of no interest to your client, and especially those that return and in which your client still has no interest.

Re-including our physiological knowing has serious implications that extend into the realm of ethics and morality. If I really let myself sense how you are at work, I almost certainly can't let myself behave in quite the same way towards you. If I sense into the experiences of those I encounter when I am a manager, a worker or a customer – or as this strange thing called 'change consultant' – I will probably learn something. It might be uncomfortable or involve some risks to comment on what I experience or work actively with it. Sensing (albeit accidentally) into that long-ago experience of being a supplier, into the attendant feelings and impulses, offered some potentially shocking data about the dynamics of the situation. Back then, I simply wasn't courageous or skilled enough to use it: now I would regard it as a core part of my practice.

Sometimes people think that I am arguing for matter-over-mind to replace the mind-over-matter mantra of the last couple of thousand years, arguing for the body to be to the fore. I mean to press for something slightly different, more subtle and perhaps more demanding. I want to propose that we re-include our bodies in our professional lives, that we take seriously the idea that we are in physical relationships with each other even if we never touch, meet or even speak. To support this, I would ask you to explore your own physical responses to an email or letter from a person you've never met.

I'd like us to take seriously the idea that we are in these physical relationships as we work together, that taking this sensory and physical experience seriously together with our intellectual, emotional and imaginal experience could be useful to us. I see a parallel between how we currently view the body in organisations and how (before the work of Steve Fineman (2000) and Daniel Goleman (1996)) we used to view emotions in organisations: a messy unfortunate by-product of being human, to be minimised or ideally ignored in the interests of getting our work done and our profits made. Might we begin to re-develop our bodily intelligence? Bodies are not some kind of ultimate arbiter of truth; but we deny ourselves an important aspect of knowing if we merely suppress the faint queasiness that stirs as we agree to undertake work that we have some doubts about, or ignore the prickle of excitement in our bellies as one particular option gets suggested in an otherwise tedious meeting.

An Evolving Practice

In my conversations with John, I found it difficult to describe what I did and how it might make for a different experience for my clients. I could set out the theoretical territory and I think I gave him some sense of my passion for this work, but still something was missing. Finally, I took the advice that I had been freely offering to Kevin in his own writing (and should clearly have been offering to myself!) and got back to practice, inviting John to come for some embodied coaching and *experience* my working. This seemed a serious demand of an editor but then John is no ordinary editor – and of course there is an interesting congruence between his generous willingness to go for this personal inquiry and the general principles of ADOC. I'd like to finish with his description of his experience because what in the end matters for me is whether the way I've developed through ADOC has the potential to make a difference for me, for my clients and the world. This is John's experience of my practice:

> We meet outside the Museum. It's shut and we go to a noisy café to talk about friends and family in a place where the music is too loud and the coffee expensive and weak. We're in my old university town, somewhere filled with ambiguous memories for me – I was meant to like it much more than I did. How I digest, people and history will be themes.

> [Me] *"I feel braced… ready for anything. I'm full of lactic acid and adrenaline. That phone call I ignored is from a neighbour, a nice chap, but my body is ready for bad news when I ring him back. 1,000 to 1 on he wants to meet for a gossip and a drink – but my body has already filled up with terror of the other and the impossible news they may bring."*

> [Sarah] *"I feel sick… in my stomach."*

> Later on we'll talk about dogs returning to their vomit and how she didn't raise it at the time. It's an image I had then and have now.

> We walk together through the botanic gardens – I pay no attention to route, going where Sarah steers me. The phone call and my reaction to it is fortuitous, it takes me into a pattern of my experience that is disturbingly honest and one I feel shameful of – talking real time about this panic, the fear of what the other may (will) bring into my life is levelling.

> Sarah takes what I speak to, getting me to break down the experience into more than the fear of the other… I speak to the need to feel safe, the need to avoid surprises and how I've created a practice that helps me keep the world at arm's length – gives me time to digest. This focus on digestion comes after the event, but now I know it, it seems obvious from the moment we started talking.

Very early on Sarah talks about her gut, her upper midriff – the feeling of acid in her stomach… the need to vomit. She asks about the intensity of the reaction in my own gut – letting me play with, take seriously or ignore the offering of her own experience of what I thought was only mine.

And writing now, after the event, I remember the work on mirror neurones that Sarah spoke to when we first met. How we are all constantly and minutely picking up the experience of the other by other than consciously copying each other's bodies.

We go on and Sarah lets me talk, saying nothing and just walking beside me. Talking is not a problem for me – I'm full of words and clever thinking, but over the time we spend together I move into wordlessness. I stay with the formlessness of experience, the unspent tears that come from sacrificing a career to bring up children, now to have them leave home. Sarah nudges me to let go of the polite formulations and managed equivocations and I talk to the childish frustration of not having the world as I want it – to having stepped off the conventional hierarchy of success and been left with the existential challenge of making a life of my own, now I'm fifty, fitting in with the plans of the youngsters who haven't taken the detours I have. The envious attacks I want to make.

In the Winter Garden we hit a blockage of students and retrace our steps and Sarah talks to her body; only then do I begin to notice the scents of the place, I've completely turned in on myself. Her responses are focused around her eyes and her stomach. I run with the eyes, taking the intellectual high ground and wondering about framings and how I see things – and there's something in this. Sarah offers a different form of reflection to that of my professional colleagues or my psychoanalyst. There is nothing to debate, no doubt as to the validity of how reality is being known. She shares what her body is up to – it is as unled a response as is possible; better than the facilitators', coaches', analysts' standby of "tell me more", she is offering me data.

Everything is offered with the possibility that what she is experiencing is what I am experiencing – she is telling me what is going through me more easily than I can know it myself. Later on when I begin to acknowledge the loss of where I've been, I'll let my eyes fill up but only a bit (it's soon bitten down: I really don't find public expressions of emotion easy – after 12 years I've yet to take advantage of my analyst's box of tissues).

The stomach ebbs and flows – she tunes in to the tone and vitality of my language, noting how when I speak with conviction about a world that is formed in the madness of fashion (rather than the fantasy of some natural scientist's laboratory or MRI scanner), her stomach unknots – but then reknots as my equivocation, doubt and burdens of duty heave back into view.

Later on when we pay attention to the nature of what we did together, she talks to the experience of making cakes with her son and how she folds in egg white to loosen the mixture – she doesn't do icing. In her work she doesn't fix people into a form or some model for knowing themselves – she doesn't insist that they unbutton themselves, she simply makes available her experience in a way that might make it possible for them to become looser. For me, this looseness is about the tightness of the gut, of holding something in that I need to expunge.

She's good at leaving the diagnosis to me – if diagnosis is what I deem to be necessary. She keeps the relational frame ambiguous and doesn't make it easy, even possible, for me to experience her as some magical other who will be the Doctor (to heal me), the Mother (to love me unconditionally) or the Lover (to make me whole). She is the embodied mirror, the one who offers the possibility of knowing myself through her, but not by becoming her or entering into one of those three magical other relationships.

She doesn't report her experience through a propositional or rationalised frame, which would invite us into some dreadfully impoverished I–It experience – instead she shares her reality, with the simple and universal language of physical sensation… the very basis of I–Thou being, the uncomplicated acknowledgement of the presence of the other through how Sarah has allowed herself to notice how she has been effected.

Walking the Edge

After some time, it might be forty minutes or so, she points out how close I always walk to the edge of the path. I've been talking about the ambiguity of belonging for a lot of the time – implicitly and explicitly. At first, she tells me, she thought it was because she wasn't giving me the space – somehow I was being squeezed, but as time passed it was always the same.

She names it as we walk along a broad reach, a path that must be four yards or so across, and I see for the first time that I am walking as close as I can to the grass border.

At her prompting I take the lead and take us onto the grass, past the ominously named Systematic Beds and then on into a knot of something less rectangular. I tell a story I often tell of feeling like a character in the movie *Spinal Tap*, the bass player who describes himself as "luke-warm water" between the poles of fire and ice represented by the two creative leads of the band. I go on to describe myself as a handmaiden to the ideas of others – something passive, almost not there, never described as a character in their own right. Sarah shares the image that comes to her mind, water as a conductor, a medium that conducts and connects the different currents of others: her sense of the role I'm playing in this latest ADOC book. I remember the active and sometimes spiky exchanges I've had with Kevin and Bill as the book got going, or the less than handmaidenly negotiations with the Ashridge Research people and their parsimonious attitude to my fee!

The feelings ebb and flow as I talk more and less freely, but Sarah's stomach continues to be the centre of her sensation, sometimes loosening up but for the most part being the centre of something tight and stuck. I know that feeling of slight and perpetual sickness – of being on the edge of some "technicolour yawn" as Sarah suggests later in the warmth of the café, surrounded by the noises of mums and their under-fives.

Just before we come to the end of the walking and talking, I lighten up for a moment, remembering fondly the comedy of Stephen Fry in *Blackadder Goes Forth*. The crassly happy general with his big gut and absolute sense of entitlement – we muse about what it is to be at one with one's gut, to enjoy and accept it as part of oneself, a privilege still available to men if not women. And then we finish on vomit and how Sarah is drawn to look into it and find out what's there. I need to purge…

Stepping Back... What I See Now about Sarah's Practice

I write as someone who is knowledgeable in this arena. I have experienced many forms of reflective relationship and have earned my living, in part, as a purveyor of the dark arts of self-knowledge. I know the mainstream and I know what lies at the outer edges and what needs a particular practice meets. I know the manipulation and hidden subjectivity of so many so-called truth peddlers.

My encounter with Sarah had distinctive qualities and gave me insight I hadn't had before. What lay behind this may be some of the following:

- *Cognitive bypass.* She made it possible for me to bypass my strongly developed cognitive habits. She helped me to connect to the strong meat of how I actually feel and construct experience, not how I'd like to feel and construct reality. She also stayed with the bypass and didn't make the rush towards some idealised 'norm', which is frequently a shorthand for trying to manipulate experience into something deemed socially valuable – a habit many cognitive-based approaches have embedded in them.

- *No premature rush to framing.* The trouble for those of us who work with people with a particular model in mind is that we inevitably nudge them towards a line of thinking that fits with our framing. As the cliché goes, to a hammer everything looks like a nail – or to a Kleinian everything looks like the splitting between the good and bad breast. Because Sarah's work stays with her bodily response, there is no framing model in action. In Heron's terms, she stays at the expressive and experiential, avoiding the premature rush to the analytical and propositional – by having no analytical or propositional to rush to. Culturally this presents a challenge as our culture values exactly that rush. I value being left to make my own sense and choose my own course of action.

- *Relational data as data about the self.* She makes it hard, near impossible, to make her one of those idealised types of rescuing relationship (Lover, Mother, Doctor). Her data is all about her body, not about the fantasy and miasma that exists in the intangible between-ness of relating. She grounds her being with you in a material and all-but-objective other – she is not speaking to what might be or what can be constructed from interpretation of behaviour. She is speaking to her 'what-isness'. The choice as to whether you see that data as a mirror of your own experience is left with you. The mirror, or rather reflective frame, she offers is one that invites you to pay attention to your own gut, eyes etc., not whether you are constructing her as some magical other. She offers relational data as self-data, rather than data about relationship.

- *Visible and accessible presence.* Sarah shows up in the encounter – she doesn't hide behind some socially approved practice, some notion of pseudo-objectivity or some other habit of claimed non-participation. What she offers is free of the horrible language of so much psychoanalytic framing, which immediately creates distance between 'expert' and client. She offers her experience as cleanly and simply as is possible, as unframed by the complications of fashion and theory as possible. Anyone can understand the data she shares. She avoids creating a hierarchy of self-knowing in which the other has some superior language or framing.

We share a common interest in the work of Carl Jung – one of the last times I'd been to this town, I'd met with a man who'd met him in Uganda in the fifties. For me, Sarah has the qualities of the Psychopomp, that paradoxical guide who invites you to engage with a path of your own making.

CHAPTER 8

A Dialogue about a Private Eye and a Public Sphere

Engaging with Sarah's work led us into a conversation about presence and the significance of having one's presence acknowledged. For some people, such as Helen Ralston, a later ADOC graduate, that takes the form of 'being heard' and their metaphor of choice involves the notion of 'voice' and 'voicing'. Other people use visual metaphors and speak of 'being seen', or more frequently 'not being seen' in their organisation. The Ubuntu greeting, a visually based metaphor par excellence, made a deep impression on me. Standing in front of a person and saying "I am here to be seen" and receiving the response "I see you" is altogether of a different quality than our habitual "Hello, how are you?" with the usual response "I am well and how are you?", however sincerely it may have been delivered. Both of us had felt seen by Steve Marshall.

John: I love Steve's work. He finds a way to show people as he sees them, in all their beauty and humanity. His pictures are potent because he gives us an image of ourselves that is not normally available to us. Seeing his picture of me, with my shoulders hunched, a man carrying a burden, was really rather disturbing. He caught an aspect of me that I'd rather not admit even to myself, let alone to anyone else. I had no idea it was so visible.

Kathleen: For me his work is like feedback, information mediated by a relationship. Steve shows us how he has experienced us in a particular moment. He's a skilled photographer, so he has the ability to create an image that really captures his experience of the person or situation in question. I think that you and I were disturbed by Steve's pictures of us for different reasons and that disturbance gave us both lots of food for thought. His work reminds me of the metaphor a Brazilian client had for action learning: it was, he said, like walking into a room full of mirrors. I was really shocked at first by Steve's picture of me and, at the same time, I was touched and fascinated. There is something deeply moving about being truly 'seen'.

John: There's something potent in the immediacy of the medium. Steve manages to bypass the sometime trickery of words. Words tend to take us into our heads, which in turn often takes us away from the present moment.

Kathleen: Gergen (1999) would say that we don't describe the world we see, rather we see the world we describe; and our Western languages tend to be particularly individualistic and mechanistic in spirit and vocabulary, thus limiting our life world. A Japanese AMOC alumna really struggled to describe her experience in English because she found the language lacking in words, especially those that pointed at the 'interpersonal'.

John: In that respect, I see a strong connection between Steve and Sarah's work. They are both interested in a way of knowing that isn't easily put into words, but is there to be seen or felt all the same. The kind of knowing that makes leading and consulting more of a craft than we like to admit. If leading is a craft then we can't learn to lead well just from reading books and manuals, just like we can't learn to ride a bicycle by merely reading about it or watching someone else do it.

Kathleen: If leading or consulting are crafts, then that means everyone who aspires to practise that craft has a responsibility to hone their skill. We're not all photographers or musicians or artists, but we all have the ability to truly see or hear someone. Helen Ralston, the ADOC graduate I mentioned earlier, dedicated her entire research to the craft of really hearing someone. She managed to hone that skill to the extent that, during a counselling meeting, a client of hers said, as he straightened his back, that he had felt "seen for the first time". The challenge is to remember the significance of this work. To be truly present for our clients or our peers requires us to be able to contain our own anxiety, resist our internal gremlins that tell us to be clever or useful, or to come up with a quick and impressive solution.

John: Let's take a look at what Steve has to say.

CHAPTER 9

Photo-dialogue: Creating the Word-image that Makes the Difference

By Steve Marshall

Introducing Steve Marshall

Last year, Facebook's 750 million users uploaded and shared 100 million photographs each day. Over 6 billion hours of video were watched each month on YouTube and 100 more hours of video were uploaded every minute. In the UK, we take more than 35 million 'selfies' every month. We both love and need our digital technology as we make, share and respond to imagery that connects us globally. The breadth of our visual reach, authority and power represents what art historian Geoffrey Batchen describes as "a sprawling cultural phenomenon inhabiting virtually every aspect of modern life."

I believe that our attempts to change and influence our organisations and workplaces are significantly extended through the use of visual techniques. Skilled practitioners can use imagery creatively to short cut the habitual, ritualised jargon that defends against change and, instead, move swiftly to meaningful conversations and relationships.

My chapter outlines some of the 'doctoral' ground that underpins my change practice. I increasingly position my work at the confluence of our current social dynamics, the easy availability of digital imagery, the nature of social media and the notion that 'aesthetic knowing' might provide simple human insight into some of our intractably complex strategic and leadership issues.

Steve Marshall

Director, Photo-Dialogue Ltd
www.photo-dialogue.com

Ashridge Faculty
www.ashridge.org

If your photographs aren't good enough, you're not close enough.

Robert Capa, Spanish Civil War photographer

If your photographs aren't good enough, you're not reading enough.

Tod Papageorge, American street photographer

Self Portrait, Steve Marshall

I think this 'selfie' is about right for now.

I constantly wonder what intervention might contribute to the change we all seem to seek.

I witness others struggling to make meaningful, generative contributions in organisations that we all wish could be vibrant, engaging and that would serve us well.

Yes, I get a bit frustrated and impatient with it at times, too.

It has taken me a while to realise that I am interested in a different kind of vision. The common requirements of business consultancy to increase profit, develop market share or become 'Number 1' seem to ring hollow in a world where we are seeing the limits of economic growth, experiencing the damage we have inflicted on our eco-system and seem to suffer from a resilient social malaise. Most of the leaders with whom I work are clear that they face seemingly impossible circumstances and what to do next is, at best, a blurry, ill-defined puzzle. Increasingly, my clients are saying, "I don't know what to do – and I have no vision of what could work." My experience on ADOC has enabled me to understand that I am interested in working with the kind of vision that will support those of us who are wrestling with these apparently impenetrable problems and, perhaps, might underpin a vision of leadership that genuinely works to improve the human condition.

It has been several years since I was seized by the moment of astonishing clarity that flashed through dappled sunlight as I drove along a wooded ridge on my way to another inconsequential change-management assignment. I remember it as a time when 'a decision took me'. Indeed, I had to stop the car and pause as the implications of the experience rattled through me. Suddenly, I had no choice; I left a guaranteed, pensionable 'job for life' and moved into the countryside with a young family and a vague intent to try a different way of working as a consultant. A year later, when I had completed the Ashridge Masters in Organisation Consulting, I still had some money in the bank but my single-minded moment of coherence had been replaced by a list of ever more challenging questions. While I had made the first step towards the kind of work that mattered to me, a much bigger transition loomed. Today I can be eloquent and I describe my quest in terms of the 'significance' of the work I choose to undertake. At that time I was left simply wondering what the hell to do with my life. Then I heard that Ashridge might be offering a doctorate along similar lines to the master's and I decided that I had unfinished business.

In Conversation with John Higgins

JH: Why that photo? [Self Portrait]

SM: It came about after a long period of reflection – after seeing your write up of our last conversation. It was also at a time when I was getting scratchy and cross, something that usually happens if I haven't done anything creative for a while. I'd been on a high after doing some visual work with [a UK-based NGO], really feeling on top of my craft, and then spent some time supervising on the Ashridge doctorate, supporting others creatively. While this is great and satisfying, it's not the same as attending to my own creativity and I'd been stuck in the office for two or three days…

I went back to what you'd written and felt bolstered by it, noticing different types of possibility and potential within both the writing and myself. I've been struggling for about a year now, too busy (ironically) to find a way to language what I do, and to present my work to the world.

Pause

I see my work as catalytic. But, because of what I do, the way I work with photography and taking pictures in the moment, I can't make any clear claims about the effect my work will have. I can describe the process, how I'll go about things, but to say "This will be the result" feels wrong. I can't, after all, predict the future. I feel that what I do can be helpful, but whether it *really* makes a difference… that's problematic for me.

So, I don't 'sell' what I do. I put offers out there, suggestions… and when one of these offers or suggestions lands with someone, I follow it up.

Back to the Photograph

What I'm trying to signify in the picture is the depth of my work, the sustained engagement I've made with the field that makes up my practice. I can find myself getting labelled as 'the bloke who does the photos' but I'm not just photos, I'm into words as well as photos. The photos provoke dialogue. So it can be either words or images, or both – without ever knowing ahead of time what word or picture is the one that will land and make some shift possible.

In the image I made in preparation for this conversation, I'm sitting on the floor. This is my natural territory. I like to take shots that are looking up at people… a flattering perspective. Sitting on the floor feels very congruent… it's how I sit when I'm working. I don't want to dominate the space where I work… which can be tricky as I'm six foot two and turn up festooned with photographic technology – which has an effect…

But on the floor I start to blend in, it feels more like I'm just hanging out with people.

JH: Could you explore this sitting on the floor a bit more?

SM: OK, this is what it feels like a lot of the time… I'm coming at things from a low angle, just looking over the tops of office desks. Sitting on the floor I become part of the background.

JH: Most consulting activity consists of pretty high-status activities… there's often, even always, some sort of status game going on…

SM: I'm conscious of that… and the cameras infer a bit of power. I can do the bolshie photojournalist thing if I need to *and then* I can switch status. Having got over the need to legitimise my role in people's workspace, I can play the low status witness and documentary maker. Perhaps the most representative image of my actual working process might be one of me showing people the playback screen on the back of the camera and asking them if they're okay with the pictures I'm making.

JH: Consultants are usually enmeshed in the power/status/hierarchy game with their clients; what you do is different. What's the nature of the social contract you have with them?

SM: Rather than talk about contracts, let me talk about boundaries – the boundary conditions between clients and consultants are not straightforward. Clients often want a great deal of overlap between the consultant and themselves. They want to know that the consultant is 'one of them'; that the consultant has done what he's proposing before and that he can promise it'll work.

In my photographically based work, I have the smallest overlap I can get away with – our boundaries just touch. I was working with a telecoms company and I know nothing of telecoms. What I was interested in was moments of personal creativity, the identity of the group and instances of 'quality' in their work. So, rather than get my validation from meeting the client's need for me to be like them, I get my sense of integrity from the knowledge of what I went through to get my doctorate. Because of the hundreds of books I've read, that are behind me and in me, the reflexive process, the endless hours spent in the integration of experience, theory and practice, I can say with confidence that in the thousandth of a second it takes to take a picture I'll have something interesting to say about creativity or identity or quality or whatever…

Finding Frame and Focus

On the floor of this office is my undergraduate dissertation, yellowed pages more than 30 years old, typewritten (no word processors in those days) with a plastic binding that has all but given up the ghost. It's title, 'The Image and the Event', referred to a critique of the photojournalism of the day but it might equally apply to how I frame my consulting and leadership coaching work. Today I focus on the way we imagine and envision strategy and how, conversely, we deal with the unfolding events of our day-to-day reality. I realise that I have, for some time, been deeply concerned with *how* we see things and the impact of that 'seeing' process on our lives.

Ironically, it has taken a while for my own sense of vision to appear. It is as though I needed to wrestle continually with the questions that held real significance for me – that I needed to be sure of my ground and to be sure that I had paid my dues. As I moved from working as a photographer/journalist, wondering about the narrative impact of imagery and how I could change the world with just the right photograph, through my 'twenty and some' years as a military fighter pilot, or now as an 'organisation consultant', my concern with the 'picture' that we share has stayed at the forefront. But since working my way through AMOC[1] and ADOC[2], another, more dialogic, conversational thread of inquiry has become equally present in my work. While imagery and vision might provide a window on the soul, we still need to talk our way through our stories and pictures. We need the words and narrative too.

---

1   Ashridge Masters in Organisation Consulting (now Ashridge Masters in Organisational Change)
2   Ashridge Doctorate in Organisation Consulting (now Ashridge Doctorate in Organisational Change)

During my ADOC inquiry, I became clear that my world has never followed the conventional narrative of telling me what is about to happen, telling me what is happening, then telling me what just happened. Instead, my experiences are more complex, they intertwine, I make sense retrospectively and my learning seems to run forward or loop backwards, conversations run concurrently and, delightfully, random stuff just arrives… So much for the linear, text-based platitudes and milestoned plans that make for our Gant-charted corporate lives. But post-ADOC, I am able to articulate my own personal process within a visually informed consulting practice that also enables clients to address the kind of complexity that informs their own lived experience as leaders, strategists and innovators.

Yet when I began to present the experience of a four-year inquiry to a doctoral audience, it rapidly became clear that academia requires a particular, rather conventional version of events. A particular, conventional literary style is required and I rubbed inelegantly against the rules. So I am writing my chapter of *The Change Doctors* as part of the thesis that never was: a braided tangle of writing and images, ideas, accounts of meetings, alongside fragments of thoughts and reflections from the conversations between John and myself. It feels real to me and reflects the way I work but I know there is also risk in this approach. When I wrote for the Ashridge publication *Organisational Consulting @ the Edges of Possibility* with the instruction to "tell your own story and say how it is to be you", it seems I got my story wrong and had to significantly edit the work. But now I'm a doctor and so I guess this version of my own story will, at last, have some authority.

The Meeting: Reflections from John's Notebook (1)

I'd been there before, the Turbine Hall of Tate Modern – working with Steve before his doctorate, exploring the edges of his insight using postcards from the gift shop. We'd also sat together as he talked about his experience of being a father and being fathered – another time, another project, same place.

I came in through an unexpected entrance, walking through sepulchral gloom and up the ramp towards the light – not seeing him when he saw me. He called out once I'd passed by, after he'd taken some photos he'd show me later. My first sight of him was a white jumper[1] with a long camera covering two-thirds of his face – the unexpected portrait painter.

Steve's relationship to the doctoral experience has not been straightforward. The ADOC process is not one of simple intellectual extension: it is, at its heart, a deeply existential experience, one that demands a degree of personal presence and examination not usually engaged with by traditional doctoral processes. The traditional academic program is not well suited to cope with inquiry that sees the personal as professional, blurring and mixing together comfortable compartments that have kept the academic discourse safe from the messiness of embodied human experience. Steve's personal tension reflected the systemic tension of seeing a doctoral process in a new way, while still connecting to its well-established and rigorous traditions.

---

1   Rather delightfully, I don't own a white jumper.

John in the Turbine Hall, Steve Marshall

I hadn't seen him and he walked on past me. John is a big guy.

Solid.

And yet he manages to arrive silently.

Speak softly… I like that.

There is a subtlety in the power he has as our editor and so here is acknowledgement of the presence and framing he provides for our writing.

Continuing the Conversation

SM: The big shock for me was what happened post dissertation. I remember the external examiner saying "Congratulations, Dr Marshall" and this provoked a real plunge into transition. What caught me out as I moved back into 'normal' life after the years of doctoral inquiry was how much was still unravelled.

With the thesis out of the way and on my wife's instructions, I threw my energy into my consulting practice. She'd seen that I had been able to do the doctoral work, something she hadn't recognised as part of my natural make-up, and was firmly of the view that "if you can do that, you can do anything". When I wondered what my next challenge might be, her request was simple. She looked me in the eye and laughed. Then she said, "OK, so make a ton of money, please!" It's been a joke ever since – as well as a helpful reminder for me that the doctorate took time, energy and finance away from other, more family-orientated pursuits.

I work very hard at making the whole business administration part seem very easy. I resent the intrusion, the compromise it can invoke. Don't get me wrong, I like the spoils and fun of a successful business – but this 'splitting' is an old pattern. In writing my thesis I was holding on to what I wanted to represent, to my sense of integrity, whilst also working with what would do an 'academic' job. Again, I began to resent the intrusion and one of the external academics noted, "You've said this thesis is about consulting. But you hardly mention it. Where's your practice?" Of course, I felt that the whole thing was about practice but I had to bite the bullet and edit to meet the academic requirements. Even if they were 'minor conditions', it felt like a huge compromise.

JH: Could you say a little more about the nature of how you experienced post-doctoral transition?

SM: I had always been really keen that a 'professional doctorate' should have some sort of practical business application but often felt a little censured among the ADOC community for using terms like 'ROI'.[1] However, I needed to achieve considerable distance from the work before I could do something businesslike with it. Only now, two years on, does it feel like I have found enough space… I'm still re-organising my office… It's also taken two years to think about going on holidays and, at last, to focus on seriously spending time with my family.

JH: It sounds like somewhere along the way you had lost your own sense of the focus?

SM: Absolutely… and my coping strategy was to fill the gap with activity. The last two years have felt headlong. I co-founded a new consulting partnership straight away after completing the doctorate. The business did well and made money, but ultimately, it was not how I saw my life unfolding. At the time, my fellow partners had considerable aspirations and saw themselves running a big organisation employing lots of associates. I guess I was seduced by the idea but neglected to attend to what I was actually doing and how it fitted with my sense of self and practice. My role became soulless: finance, performance indicators, IT and business control. I was the one with an MBA and while I think I can do that kind of thing well, it's not how I choose to make my contribution.

Those years were a salutary experience. I really had not appreciated how long it would take for work and identity to settle. My own vision for my work was immature and I needed to ground what a more aesthetically informed, artful practice might mean. The thesis had been a way of sketching out that territory; turning it into a sustainable practice takes time… is taking *me* time.

---

1   Return on Investment

Obsession and Optimism

Fighter pilots obsess over the 'picture': the dynamic, unfolding image of the high-speed, high-stakes, tactical manoeuvring and action that constitute their worlds. The picture emerges from a synthesis of careful pre-briefing and rehearsal, radar imagery, the voice of a ground controller, aircraft and weapon capability, visual sightings and often-screamed inter-cockpit instructions. As the immediate tactical scenario emerges, situational awareness forms, strategy develops and action follows. Back on the ground, we would endlessly replay our 'tapes' to understand what each of us had seen during the mission and how effective our collective efforts had been.

Such was the backdrop to my flying career and while today's pace of life, even in the most hectic client engagements, is more considered, opportunities to reflect on the nuance of life and practice can feel rare. There are no 'tapes' of my experience and the data is often incomplete, biased or simply forgotten. Yet I realise that I still operate like a fighter pilot, on a mixture of half-held hunches, an over-optimistic assessment of my chances of success and an unreasonable belief in my own ability. There are consequences to this kind of attitude and I recall the cartoonist Hugh MacLeod[1] offering some kind of anchor point: "I work extremely hard doing what I love, mainly to ensure that I don't have to work extremely hard doing what I hate." With this in mind, returning back to the yellowed pages of 'The Image and the Event' feels like a re-engagement with an artefact that continues to offer questions and inspiration for work that is a life-long calling.

Perhaps there was something of this sentiment rattling around my head as I arrived at Ashridge for my ADOC acceptance interview. I explained to faculty members Kathleen King and Robin Ladkin (who would both later become much-valued colleagues) that, rather than resolving questions of practice, AMOC had asked more, and that doing a doctorate would actually be less troublesome than not doing one. It was the best rationale that my 'work hard doing what you love' script could describe.

If AMOC had encouraged me to formulate a practice that offered a framing of decision making and strategy through the lenses of complexity, improvisation and dialogue, I had hoped that ADOC would enable me to research an experience of organisational relationships seen aesthetically. I guess that an image of the past friendships and the close bonds of a fighter squadron was a clear, if unseen, point of reference as I began an inquiry into how relational quality might be an indicator of organisational performance.

1   Cartoonist, author and Internet publisher Hugh MacLeod: http://www.gapingvoid.
     com

Considering the Work

JH: If we begin to look more clearly at your practice, I'm still intrigued by the power that minimal overlap makes possible, compared to that of maximal overlap. What makes it possible for you to work with such a limited degree of familiar connection?

SM: Mmmm… What happens in those moments of photography? There's an essence of reality… People see a form of truth in a photo, there is a particular sense of relationship to the image. Working from a photograph, taken in an instant as I sit on the floor and they go about their work, we can then talk much more easily about some of the previously invisible, tacit dynamics that structure their context and relationships. People often don't feel these things are important enough to talk about because they don't count as a task or something that fits within the implicit assumption of what is valid 'knowing' within the business organisation.

The Red Fingernail of Detail, Steve Marshall

I was fascinated by the way these colleagues worked together.

Their conversation had an almost rhythmic song-like quality as they set out possibility, boundaries, rigour and focused their attention.

That red fingernail became an emblem for the whole organisation: "We design well; we take our stuff very seriously."

What my way of working makes possible is the capacity to have meaningful conversations more quickly. The imagery is designed to extend the range of what we normally count as organisational 'data' and enables a different kind of relational conversation. I guess that, ultimately, 'creativity' is my field and I need to be able to help people talk fluently about the nature of creativity in organisations. I have to be skilled at getting these conversations going because they are not the normal conversations my clients have. I've used the Ashridge Doctorate to learn how.

In the pictures I take there will always be some sort of truth, some 'red fingernail of detail' that kick-starts the conversation, that builds fast, deep rapport in the consulting relationship. With rapport and resonance made possible by the picture, and the learning I've brought to that moment, we can really pay attention to what each of us see in the here and now of the image.

JH: What is distinctive about the conversations you have with people now compared to those you had before the doctorate?

SM: Conversations go faster and deeper. We get into relevant material much more easily.

JH: Why do you think this is?

SM: Let me give you an example; I want to show you something that took me by surprise [Steve reaches for his iPad]. I got some feedback when I did the [NGO] work. Before the start of the workshop, I'd asked the group to each take digital pictures that spoke to their professional practice and then send it to me. I printed them to a really high standard and handed them out as I began to set out our work. I had asked that we would use the pictures to start to our work together; I wanted to use the visual images to set the dialogic 'container' and we got into interesting stuff straight away.

But now the feedback… "An amazingly fresh perspective… Fantastic delivery, charisma and trust… Steve's not worried about using the correct terminology – more concerned about what *we're* saying… Very thought provoking". And so on. I can do this because we connect quickly through imagery and, as you can see from the background of my own picture, with all those wretched books, I guess I know my stuff!

In terms of process, I can take a snippet of the client's reality, a photograph, and then the person is differently present in the conversation. I can use their material and I'm not getting in their way – because I'm not expert in their field. In my own field, I'm very expert… but that's invisible to them… so when I turn up in someone's offices or place of work, the technology of photography means I'm actually in my own backyard, I'm on my ground and I can go wherever they want to go.

JH: I'm very taken with the idea of consultants having their own ground…

SM: It's a challenge to, or a reframing of, the traditional idea of meeting the client where they are. I remember an old *HBR* article about a Stanford Professor who explicitly tells groups when he meets with them: "I will not be relevant… finding relevance, that's your work."

He also made no judgments about what his clients did; he provided just a minimal hook to generate a learning conversation between consultant and client. The hook between me and the world of my clients might be a thousandth of a second – and as a result of that fraction they will become manifest in the image I make.

JH: You're really seeing them.

SM: Well, yes… but I'm not matching expertise in the business sense… but we're meeting at the level of… the dimension of… human contact and identity.

JH: I'm thinking with a military hat on and the meaning of the salute… with its visible statement of 'I see you'… In your work, you're seeing people, acknowledging them and their existence.

SM: I work with a different focus to traditional practitioners in the field of organisational aesthetics – I tend to find the work there a bit of a turn off. Most of organisational aesthetics seems to be concerned with the shape of the speakerphone or the colour of the wallpaper and I'm just not interested in that sort of thing.

I'm interested in the aesthetic of organisational relationships… trying to find a way of bringing into the frame the aesthetics of relating within a particular setting. That's why portraits fascinate me! If I go back to the pictures of the people in the telecoms company, there's the guy who's lost in his world… I'm fascinated by the prospect of capturing that quality of engagement.

I think my portraits are simply appreciative images of people in their working contexts. I try to capture moments when people are expressing something amazing. I can point to them being at their best in their work and then I can ask, appreciatively, who is *this* person?

Lost in a World, Steve Marshall

I do this too.

I get lost in my world, a kind of 'flow' state where time stops and my concentration is entirely complete.

The question though is how can we structure our organisations to enable this kind of process to happen more often?

Defining Form

We are, of course, almost constantly surrounded by different sorts of visual technologies – photography, film, digital graphics, television, acrylics, for example – and the images they show us – TV programmes, advertisements, snapshots, Facebook pages, public sculpture, movies, closed circuit television footage, newspaper pictures, paintings. All these different technologies and images offer views of the world; they render the world in visual terms.

(Rose, 2012: 2)

Many writers make the claim that the visual is central to our experience, the most fundamental of all senses. In my undergraduate days, I remember John Berger (1972: 7) suggesting that "seeing comes before words. The child looks and recognises before it can speak." In making the visual element of our experience integral to my practice, I aim to open up and legitimise other ways of 'knowing' within our organisations and lived experience. Photographs are particularly useful to me in this respect; the camera phone and similar digital technologies are ubiquitous in our lives and our knowledge of the world, through established media or newer, 'social' forms, is increasingly articulated visually.

Photo-Elicitation

John provided my first exposure to photo-elicitation when I was at a 'stuck' point during my master's degree. We met at the Tate Modern and bought art cards from the gift shop, choosing them on the basis that they simply appealed to us, and then took turns to spread our collections out on the floor of the Turbine Hall. John asked me to tell the story of my consulting practice using the cards I had purchased. I was completely shocked by the words that came out of my mouth as I articulated a practice unlike any of the other models of consulting or coaching I had experienced.

One particular image has lived with me ever since: Sandy Skoglund's 'Red Foxes Out to Lunch', a bizarre scene where grey people in a grey restaurant seem oblivious to the fact that the restaurant is overrun with red foxes jumping over the tables and chairs. For me, the red foxes seemed to symbolise a mischievous sense of the emotion and energy that grey organisations fail to recognise.

Organisational Reportage

Working with a reportage brief is a luxury. In this kind of work I am following a contract devised with the client to look appreciatively for particular moments of relationship that would provide a prompt for dialogue into, for example, the conditions that might promote or provoke organisational change and innovation – or, as in the example below, how we might lead and co-operate effectively by listening well and fully attending to those around us.

This image appeared as I wandered around a workshop where participants had been given a brief to interview each other. It was a productive, buzzy interlude for a group that were otherwise often dispersed or working on different shifts. The opportunity to meet and work together felt like a special moment that I wanted them to remember. The purpose behind these images is both to witness and to honour the subjects, and to provide a spur for inquiry among participants. So I might be asking something along the lines of "Is this what collaboration looks like?" or "How could we get more of this?"

Collaborative Images

Kevin sent me a photograph that a friend had made of him as they walked in Highgate Cemetery. I was instantly intrigued. I've known Kevin for several years and he brings a somewhat elusive and mysterious sense of presence to his practice. I see him as deeply experienced and rather powerful in the way he 'comes alongside' his clients and their organisations.

He manages to 'hold' group and organisational processes as a 'whole' rather than breaking them down into their constituent parts and I know this takes enormous effort and concentrated attention. I find his method curiously artistic and wanted to extend his image to that of a rather troubled philosopher or academic, so I cropped the picture to provoke the viewer's attention and increased the contrast to achieve a heightened sense of drama.

I imagine that the appearance of Karl Marx in this image is not an accident. It would have been easy for me to place it in the frame using Photoshop or similar software: yet, as with any dialogic conversation, whilst there is a need to suspend and hold back fantasy, sometimes 'the random stuff' makes its presence felt!

Photo-Projections

This is a process where I engage in a visual conversation with the client in (usually) a coaching environment. As we began to imagine how we might be 'showing up' as consultants in the early stages of producing this book, I started to work up images of my colleagues.

My process with this kind of work is to let my projections and fantasies run free – as I work with the pictures, I am able to 'Photoshop' and digitally manipulate the photo to my heart's content. The resultant image becomes a conversation piece; my projections of the 'client' play out and I offer them in an artistic spirit of inquiry. When the client sees the image, their projections and fantasies also come into play. In most conventional coaching conversations, this kind of material works away in our unconscious processes. My aim is to bring this material, which is at the basis of our human relating, artfully and often playfully to the fore.

Kathleen simply asked me to make an image when she was working at a conference. I had heard her describe her work as "just meetings, really" and I felt that I would challenge that particular self-deprecatory version of her practice.

There is a bit of pop-star glamour going on here for me, though the wrinkles around her eye hint at the depth and experience Kathleen brings to her work. I initially thought I might smooth them away – but didn't and duly endured the complaints! The deeper appreciation of Kathleen as a leader of ADOC remains and, I think, confronts some of her own denial of the agency of her role.

More than meets the eye

Co-constructed Imagery

Perhaps my most rewarding work takes place when I work with a client as we both enter the struggle of extending our sense of 'knowing' and together devise an image that begins to explore issues where words are ineffective. When I worked with Carla, she immediately said that she did not want to be photographed. We were inquiring into the nature of invisible, seamless 'service' and the quality of the working relationship that such a concept implies.

Yet we agreed that I would photograph her in a way that would be representative of her sense of anonymity. As Carla prepared one of the coffee bars that would

be her responsibility for the day, I set the camera and began to make a series of images. We needed to find just the right amount of invisibility: where she could be polite and responsive to guests whilst also maintaining a respectful distance should she detect that the guest needed space for contemplation or peace.

Participative Visual Inquiry

As much as possible, I try to hand the cameras over to the clients and participants. This is an important inversion of the normal power relationship invoked by a photographer 'taking' a picture.

If this is not possible, I invite them to be 'art director' as I tend to the technical issues and then bring them fully into the selection and editing process. In this gallery process, the group is taking part in a visual variation of 'Appreciative Inquiry'. They are voting for images by putting stickers on them and using post-its or simply writing straight onto the images to record ideas that came to mind as a result of the work. The inquiry moved on from 'This is what creativity looks like...' to the structural and relational changes that would be required to support creativity and innovation in their organisation. It was a conversation that would have been problematic in a more conventional form.

What Changes?

JH: Tell me how it works as an organisational intervention.

SM: What I think I offer people is a way of being seen. Rather than the military salute, I think of the Zulu greeting... "I see you" and the response "I am here".

Many organisations make people invisible, or at least they make a large part of their lives invisible. I allow people to be present and be witnessed... and when that happens they open up and you have very different conversations with them about what they bring to their work, how they show up. My best pictures honour people.

JH: I'm aware of how different what you do is to much organisational practice... you're seeing individuals not units of production.

SM: I'm seeing people as creative, valuable, beautiful and vital.

JH: If people really are an organisation's greatest asset then the first step you take as a senior manager is to see them as magnificent people. So much organisational language kills the presence of the individual.

SM: A while ago, I made this image of a guy working a printing machine. He was clearly very skilled and I loved the craft he brought to his work... there was a care and attention to what he did. I think of craft as being about something that you can never reduce away, an ability that can't be easily transferred. His craft came from years and years of being around printing. The picture I took really honours him. His manager took his picture, along with several others, and put them up in reception. It was a simple gesture but it provided a shift in organisational identity, a 'this is who we are' that was immediately visible to clients and visitors.

The visual process enabled something to happen. I had a long conversation with him about the nature of printing as a craft. It was a hundred-year-old firm and there was a lot of vintage machinery around. As we talked he told me "I've got a job to do and we'll use an old machine." As he worked, it looked pretty ferocious with metal flying everywhere: "We don't normally do this but it's great to go back to it!" I was fascinated. He was literally making the tool to do the job. It was amazing to have a conversation with someone who'd done this printing job all his life and to explore with him the nature of his craft and what he was bringing to the organisation.

Craftsman, Steve Marshall

I'm in awe of people who can still do 'real work'.

One of the attractions of my own photographic craft is that I can actually give people something to take away with them as part of the intervention.

And I love it when they say, "Wow!"

JH: My daughter has just finished reading a Richard Sennett book, *The Culture of the New Capitalism* (Sennett, 2006), where he revisits much of his thinking about craft. He highlights how the consulting industry has no capacity to value in-depth, hard-earned craft. The focus is on the capacity to acquire new skills not deepen existing ones. By valuing the craft of this man in the print shop you're valuing the person. I'm wondering if what you're touching on is the craft of being a good human being… is there such a craft?

SM: I would say there is. After the doctorate, I take the reflective process around this very seriously. It's raised questions about what I'm prepared to do with my life and who I'm prepared to be in the world. Where I've got to, and it sounds so corny, is that the purpose in the images I take and work I do with them is to bring witness to the lives of other people – that's the work I can do and should be doing. This is a calling for me and the question is how do I, and others, become good at our calling?

Lots of photographers do their best stuff when they get a bit older… there is a new confidence and the technical aspects disappear. A lot of my work as a young man was derivative. Now I blend this activity with my academic work, which I struggle with… I struggle to be an academic in the traditional sense… I'm not interested in knowledge for its own sake. But I'm crafting a practice from academia and this practice is about working with the creativity of others. I want to make this practice my space.

The Power of Tangible Transitional Objects: Reflections from John's Notebook (2)

For me, Steve's work is the antithesis of much of the excessively rational and worded work of consultants, which hardly ever does anything but take excitement and vitality out of the client–consultant encounter. His work seems to be in the service of what economists refer to as the animal spirits of ambition and creative expression – the messy, energising material that doesn't look good in a two-by-two matrix or PowerPoint presentation, but without which none of the rational disciplines have any meaning or momentum.

It isn't just the transitional capability of the photos; they also provide something physical and tangible. Steve finds it difficult when coaching/consulting with no physical artefact or 'thing' to give away: there's something ancient or basic in the social habit of giving and receiving gifts. There is also something about the intention behind the photo. Steve is resolute in the intention behind his work as a way of honouring people's experience. It is about seeing people well and with positive regard – this was an important part of his thesis. Steve describes his orientation to the world as having a "Zen-like fascination with the beauty of potentially mundane things." As I made my notes, I noticed that he had become fascinated with the patterns of my pencil shavings – I take my notes during interviews using soft-leaded pencils that need frequent sharpening.

Steve has the capacity to find beauty in the ordinary. This is in contrast to a world where so much is seen as not good enough. Maybe Steve's interest in beauty is connected to this capacity for seeking out the good enough, that which can be honoured and appreciated – which in turn will create a form of relationship and connection that will put his consulting and coaching work on a very different footing to a traditional, deficit-based practice.

What Photography Makes Possible

JH: I wonder if your photography helps slow your clients down so they can be more attentive to a situation?

SM: Yes, and I work with photography simply because I can't paint or draw! I'm trying to pay attention to details and the specifics of the relational context. Using photography, I can draw people's attention to things in ways I couldn't otherwise.

I took some pictures of guys working in new product development… I found myself intrigued by the creative moments of conflict. It was all but invisible, and was certainly deniable if I'd referred to the dynamic after the event. But the group was used to me photographing them and I got some beautiful shots of people in confrontation in this meeting… so subtle, but it pushed them to speak to those moments.

Advocacy, Steve Marshall

A brief moment.

This confrontation was over before it had begun, dissolving into laughs and smiles.

But the point was well made and the conflict was genuine.

It is in these moments where the power in relational configuration is challenged and real innovation becomes possible.

JH: It seems that your practice is about is 'offering the moment' in a way that has beauty about it.

SM: Beauty is helpful. I can use a picture like this to pose the question "What does creativity look like in this organisation?" and be confident of a very different quality of insight to that which would arise if I simply said "Tell me about creativity in this organisation."

JH: If I go back to the picture you took before I knew I'd walked past you in the Turbine Hall, I was struck by my being in the half-light, someone who lives in the shadows – exactly what it feels like when I'm engaged in this sort of inquiry, where I'm present with those I'm meeting but also not present. The picture is undoubtedly your story, not mine, but I'm in it a bit, somewhere in the penumbra where I feel most comfortable.

Academic, Consultant, Artist

My initial sense of originality and academic contribution took a knock as soon as I found out that the field of 'organisational aesthetics' was alive and well without any input from me! But, as I read, I became frustrated with the tedious nature of much of what I found on the library shelves. An intellectual engagement with organisational aesthetics seemed to lead me towards dry texts that analysed the function of the various artefacts found in modern workplaces.

There were, however, some glimpses of hope from kindred spirits. In her work on writing as a method of inquiry, Laurel Richardson observes:

> I have a confession to make. For 30 years, I have yawned my way through numerous exemplary qualitative studies. Countless numbers of texts have I abandoned half read, half scanned. I'll order a new book with great anticipation – the topic is one I'm interested in, the author is someone I want to read – only to find the text boring. Recently, I have been 'coming out' to colleagues and students about my secret displeasure with much of quality writing, only to find a community of like-minded discontents.

> (Richardson, 1994: 516)

I get the impression that the Action Research community has moments when it begins to make a dent in the normal, staid academic traditions, but then seems to retreat again as the wider circumstances dictate. While I realised that my inquiry could never be held in a conventionally positivist framing of organisational consulting and hoped that ADOC's Action Research approach offered the possibility of re-writing the rules, it would clearly not be straightforward. However, I clearly needed to work with an institution offering a research paradigm that would allow me to develop my own artistic as well as academic capabilities:

> There is an important specification which rules out any equivalence between the aesthetic approach and the passive reception of organisational life. Aesthetics is an aid to observation, notes Odo Marquard (1989), and as such it is antithetical to *anaesthetica*, which means putting people to sleep; an outcome, according to

Marquard, that aesthetics can also achieve. How, by transforming sensitivity into insensitivity, and art into somnolence by anaesthetising reality. Researchers who analyse organisational life using the aesthetic approach, therefore, must begin by arousing and refining their own sensory and receptive faculties.

(Linstead and Höpfl, 2000: 17)

Yet it still feels like there is potential for ridicule as I push myself to make my creative offerings and interpretations more widely available in both academic and commercial environments. 'Being creative' is a role that is rarely taken seriously and it feels like the wider academic institutions are attempting to impose hard, quantitative measures and thus squeeze out any sense of creative difference. Thankfully, as Ashridge is an independent business school, we have some autonomy and I can fall back on my sense of integrity and what I know to be valuable in professional practice.

There have been many calls to conduct inquiry into the more sensory and less rational sides of organisational reality. Taylor and Hansen (2005: 1,227) ask aesthetically informed inquirers to be "trained researchers and exploratory artists". They note that, "We see the use of artistic forms to look at these fundamentally aesthetic issues to have the potential to finally bring these important areas into the mainstream of organisational research and practice."

So, while I find the academic justification for my organisational practice heartening, I am most attracted by the mischief of writers like Laura Sewall, who (perhaps with a nod to my wife) elegantly frames the realities of an arts-based creative practice: "Artists, we presume, live on some faulty edge of reality, poets are essentially unrealistic, sensualists are not to be taken seriously, and, by the way, can't you make a little money?" (Sewall, 1999: 81)

Coffee Break

JH: Where are you now?
SM: I'm getting increasingly serious about craft, which is an orientation towards my ongoing developmental work that I find helpful.
JH: Because...
SM: It legitimises what I'd seen as self-indulgent. The discipline and practice of going off and reading the texts that I really enjoy, rigorously developing my organisational practice and taking pictures. Calling it 'craft' has a magical connotation, a kind of wizardry that touches on the subversive element in what I do. I realise that, as someone invested in change, I am both working with and being in conflict with organisations.
JH: Why is part of you in conflict with organisations?
SM: Well, I don't think I was particularly in conflict until quite late in my military career. Although the military is something big, my immediate organisation was very small. The stakes were high in what we did and not much was hidden – we were mostly concerned with doing a good job and staying alive. There was something of the purity of

the warrior, an honesty and integrity, and we worked bloody hard at looking after each other.

After a promotion, I found myself in the HQ. Suddenly I was subject to politics, oppression and a different way of organising – very similar to the process in a normal business organisation. I became disappointed at my inability to make much of a difference. I also knew I was becoming quite subversive in order to get the job done… the formal organisational processes were getting in the way of doing the work. It was also clear that rank and status were an issue. Out in the field, up against the real work, this hadn't mattered. But in the HQ, I felt that the organisational politics and processes created a distorted form of exploitative relationship between people… and I decided that kind of environment was not my thing. And I needed to do something about it…

JH: What's the difference you want to make to the lives of people you work with?

SM: I really want them to show up, to be fully present… absorbed and excited by their work – and also to contribute towards great, supporting relationships. It seems to me that when we can get this right, work stops being difficult; rather, it becomes creative and fun. Enabling people is what I'm about and this is how I reconcile my work with organisations whose outputs I'm ambivalent towards. My craft focuses on the relationships between people within the organisation.

JH: What advice would you give me about the craft of editing this book?

SM: What I hope for you is that your voice will be fully present… that you find a way of expressing your story, telling it in a way that is coherent and authentic to you. Take a few risks… be present in the work… even if you do make your place in the shadows.

JH: How do you want to show up in this book?

SM: How can I show up without spotlighting myself? I don't appear in most of the photos I take… It's good to have influence and power but my work is more to be the witness, not the witnessed.

JH: What's the title of your section?

SM: Something around the sense of being seen but not the focus. I need a title that talks to enabling people to be seen, but not by being the see-er. When I'm working, showing people's images to them, they are the see-er and the seen. I'm inviting people into reflexivity.

JH: How about 'The Seen and the Seer'?

SM: Does that sounds 'doctorly' enough? 'Witch-doctorly', maybe?

A Closing Reflection, a Final Image

Our process of working together, as a doctoral cohort, as we have assembled the writing for this book has been curiously fragmented. When we were hard into the doctoral inquiry process, Robin Ladkin ran a tight ship and Jill, Sarah, Kevin and I would, without fail, join him to make space, meet and work together. Now, however, it seems that we are involved in various professional projects, have different family and social demands and, like many of our clients, are subject to the chaotic forces of the business world. Perhaps the window for our co-inquiry opened in a timely and generous way but has now started to close again.

In a grabbed conversation at Ashridge, Sarah and I briefly compared notes about the process. She had read my draft chapter and, with a rather knowing smile, said "and there's not enough of you in it!" Her point landed well. Throughout my inquiry, I had struggled to 'show up' in my work to the extent that my colleagues demanded. As I wrestled with the notion of further explications of my embryonic creative processes, I remember complaining that "my guts are already on the floor… !" I was showing pictures of myself, my family, my home,

Portrait: Steve Marshall, Al Moffat

Al, a previous client and now good friend, took this photograph during a lighting test.

He calls it the 'Warlord' picture.

As he too is an ex-military man, I can forgive the analogy but the implications for the framing of the consulting relationship remain.

my inquiry, my practice… what else could possibly be required? Working with the images, I am deeply conscious that what is on the screen or on the page is as much a reflection of what is 'in here' as what is 'out there'. I recall once more my final viva and the challenge from one of the external examiners that I had not properly explored the nature of my consulting practice. In my response, I tried to evoke the notion of the fish in the water: practice, in terms of identity and the way consultants might 'show up', imbued everything I had offered.

Perhaps if I have not 'shown up' sufficiently for my colleagues in this writing it is because I have offered John's voice in addition to my own. As I continue to refine my work, I am aware that I am often touched by 'others' who catalyse a significant shift in both my thinking and practice. The conversation and dialogues with John, irregular as they are, always seem to provide that kind of 'nudge'. And so, if I 'write myself in' to a greater degree, I risk writing 'others' out in a way that feels deeply incoherent with my work.

So here is my final offer: a portrait that begins to hint at some of the deeper power dynamics within my practice.

As I turn my focus inwards, I imagine a character finding little attraction in the glare of the spotlight and who occupies a liminal, peripheral space. He looks out of the shadows, focusing on the illumination of a distant scene. So, finally, I realise that I am much clearer now about how I show up in client systems – and I don't make the mistake of always correlating power and leadership with visibility.

CHAPTER 10

A Dialogue about Suspending Judgement against all Odds

Both John and I have direct experience of working with Kevin Power, as a consultant and as a member of faculty on AMOC. Our conversation about that experience surfaced how difficult it can be to put into practice what we advocate. This dialogue explores some of those challenges.

Kathleen: I have often experienced Kevin's ability to slow down a process. It is both awesome and uncomfortable. On occasions I may want to move on, to make a final decision, when I notice Kevin looking a little quizzical. I know what's coming: "Can we just think about that some more?" he'll say, or "Well, I'm not sure". I sometimes dread that look. Of course, in that moment I don't think of my compulsion to act as a 'defence against anxiety'. Quite the contrary, I could most probably offer any number of convincing (sounding) reasons why it's appropriate to move on. Just as my clients, I have deadlines, a busy calendar and a finite amount of time. But when I slow myself right down and really pay attention to what is going on, I find that my sense of urgency is not quite as rational as I would like to believe and my desire for action may well be related to the uncomfortable realisation of the full complexity of the decision or the situation. So I often end up agreeing to some more thinking, even if it feels like hard work, because I know from experience that the decision we end up with is better for it.

John: We've been rather critical about contemporary leaders' 'defences against anxiety' and their tendency to treat adaptive challenges as technical ones. From what you just said, I deduce that you know what it's like, but are learning to resist the urge to flee into action prematurely. What's the pay off? What do you think Kevin is after when he presses his 'pause button'?

Kathleen: Firstly he's inviting us to consider the wider context. It can be very tempting to narrow one's focus in the midst of a problem-solving process, the famous process of 'drilling down' (another mechanistic concept in management language). Kevin will contribute to that process for a while and then, just as I think we've got to the root of the issue, he'll invite us to step right back or – to stay with the up and down metaphor – to lift our gaze to scan the horizon. Of course, when you take the context of the issue you are working on into account, you can better see the limitations and potential unintended consequences of the direction you were about to follow.

John: In Kevin's curating metaphor, that would be the equivalent of paying attention to the rooms as well as the artefacts; the colour and shape of the walls, the shape and size of the rooms, the position of doorways, the lighting, the juxtaposition of artefacts.

Kathleen: That's right. The position of artefacts in the space and in relation to one another significantly impacts our experience of them. One can think of this in terms of the Gestalt notion of figure and ground. As humans we are compelled to make sense of what we observe. Casement (2002: 110) argues that from birth we structure our experience by linking like with like: "The unfamiliar is examined in its strangeness until some sense of it can be attained. Or it is turned away from as uninteresting or as threatening, as there can sometimes be a deep disquiet when we are faced by something that is unfamiliar". In our sense-making process we tend to relegate much of the available data to the background, because it is unfamiliar or threatening, whilst we focus our attention on what has apparent meaning or is familiar, which then becomes figural. Once a figure has formed, it can be exceedingly difficult to let go of it and constitute a new figure, or return our attention to the information we had relegated to the background.

Kevin is dedicated to exploring the background, to what doesn't usually get attention, the 'back office'. Thus he goes to listen to people who don't often get a good 'listening to' and, to return to the curating metaphor, sheds light on their experience. He finds ways to connect people who may not usually be connected within the organisation and in doing so he "changes the nature of the conversation", as Patricia Shaw (2001) puts it.

John: That's an important skill for a change agent: not to be bedazzled by what is figural and in the spotlight, but to light up the background. Lighting is an important tool for a curator too, of course. Kevin is particularly skilled at surfacing important information that was hitherto ignored or considered irrelevant. His questions often concern taken-for-granted assumptions or the human aspect of a situation.

Kathleen: There is another aspect of his attention, which I have found to be invaluable. Our Newtonian legacy has trained us well to look for what is readily identifiable and to isolate component parts to work with. I'd like to use medicine as a metaphor because it seems absolutely to the point. In Western medicine, we are concentrating on the [diseases of] organs, bones, blood vessels, the tangible components of the body. They form the basis on which many of our medical specialisms are organised. Moreover, the more advanced the specialism, the smaller the part of the body it tends to be concerned with. Chinese medicine is based on a system of energy networks which, until recently, were not visible or tangible. A Chinese doctor is interested in restoring a healthy energy flow within the body and will take the context of the person, even the geographical context and the seasons, into account when deciding on a course of treatment.

John: I am particularly interested in the difference between focusing on tangible parts versus intangible 'energy flow'. In an organisational context, that would amount to paying attention to what is happening in relationships, for instance, or to the systemic dynamic, rather than zooming in on individuals, departments, structures and so on. Kevin's approach is eminently congruent with Gregory Bateson's perspective, who is one of Kevin's most significant influences.

Kathleen: Bateson wrote extensively about the significance of the 'pattern that connects' and the importance of being interested in the pattern, rather than in individual components. It is remarkable how strong a particular dynamic in an organisation can be. I have seen occasions where a 'dysfunctional' manager was replaced by a person with a very different track record and personality, only for that person to start behaving in as dysfunctional a manner as his predecessor. Even replacing an entire executive board can sometimes fail to change an organisational culture.

John: The pattern that connects, indeed. It is the toughest call for any change agent in my experience: to look beyond the tangible for the elusive; to remain always interested in the unfolding dynamic in an ever-wider net of connections.

Kathleen: It requires (most of) us to break with a socialisation pattern of a lifetime. It means we need to resist the temptation to plunge for premature solutions in an attempt to regain a sense of certainty, however much pressure we may experience to move on. It also means paying diligent attention to the present moment, which includes our embodied experience, as our thoughts are so prone to take us into the past or the future. It means that we have to engage others, and not just the usual suspects, in a dialogue so that we gain some understanding of the dynamic in the wider system. That is why Action Research is our methodology of choice and that is why it becomes a way of life.

CHAPTER 11

Curating the Curator

By Kevin Power

> If Microsoft Word ever recognised the word 'curating' it would make me a little bit sad. The world of trying out, testing new attitudes, rethinking, and pushing boundaries would freeze in that particular moment. No longer 'becoming'. No more room left.

(Maria Hlavajova in Kuoni, 2001: 82)

In recent years, the role of the curator seems to have spread beyond its traditional context of a person who would care for, catalogue and organise the display of artistic, historic or scientific artefacts. Nowadays, we are more likely to see the role as more about the idea of creating new ways of engaging audiences with artefacts of cultural interest. For example, beyond galleries, archives and museums, we now have 'curators' of festivals and programmes that showcase music, film, technology and other media or art forms. These are the people who oversee the selection of content as well as the conceptual frame that guides the *design* of the experience.

Arguably, curators are often seen as of equal cultural importance to the artists they *re*-present or as artists in their own right. It is as if the curatorial act is being reconsidered as an art form in itself. Whilst we can see or experience the end product of curating, what lies behind the act of including and excluding, of reframing and reordering, of deconstructing and reconstructing, of laying-out and of re-imagining remains elusive.

My own experience and what emerged from my research was that the curatorial act is a deeply personal process and is necessarily concerned with the political, the social, the ecological, the aesthetic and what we might call 'the existential'. It is concerned with new ways of seeing universal themes whilst also pushing the boundaries of acceptability. It is often about working at the edge. Paradoxically, curators carry an obligation to bring some kind of order and coherence to what can seem to have infinite and unbounded qualities. Yes, they are there to disturb and provoke but they are also there to help us to make some kind of sense.

For me, curating remains an ephemeral idea – it resists easy definition – and yet my doctoral research revealed remarkable similarities between the art and practice of the curator and how I think and go about my work as an organisational consultant. As an analogy and as a metaphor it has been revelatory. As one curator said to me: "The finished product is never the finished thing; just another step to formulating the next idea." This resonated with me because at the heart of my practice is an innate restlessness: never wanting to pin things down too much, nor wanting to be pinned down. It was revelatory because it suggested to me that I could be more accepting of my own 'patterns of ambivalence' as an essential ingredient in my practice rather than something that has to be overcome.

I am, however, of no use to a client unless I can bring moments of pragmatism and order. I see my consulting role as supporting the process of deepening awareness for long enough so as to enable insights that can lead to new possibilities, a deeper resolve or more intuitive (some might call it 'wiser') decision making. My intention for this chapter was to provide some kind of order and at the same to convey this emergent, restless quality. It is a never-ending work in progress. As I finalise this chapter, my thinking is already moving on.

> I find it reassuring to think of my practice as constantly in a flux of 'becoming'. For me, when there is 'no more room left' then it will be time to do something else.

(Power, 2010a: 137–8)

The Exhibition Begins

When works of art have been curated for exhibition, the final[1] act of the curator is often the creation of a brochure that previews what the visitor to the gallery space is about to experience. This chapter starts with an extract from a guided tour of the rooms in a metaphorical gallery that became the 'containing frame' for my final thesis: 'The Consultant as Curator'. It was written in a third-person style as if I am critiquing somebody else's work. I was viewing my own inquiry into my consulting practice through the lens of the 'curatorial eye'.

---

1   Or so it seems. In some cases, the iconic image that is used for marketing materials is often chosen before the curator has finalised the design of the exhibition. Some curators told me that being forced to make this premature decision can often change the way they think about the overall concept and layout.

Preview of 'The Consultant as Curator'

What do William Blake, Gregory Bateson, curating, ambivalence and aesthetic engagement have to do with the practice of organisational consulting?

What can we learn from a practitioner who persists with an inquiry approach that juxtaposes these and other phenomena in a way that is synonymous with the patterns of his own consulting method?

What does it mean to stand in your own ground whilst holding on to a vocational sense of purpose for your practice?

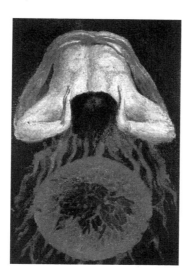

"One thought fills immensity"

An Experiment

This doctoral thesis was an experiment in form and pattern – a representation of the idea of practice as a vocational possibility... or maybe that should be: a vocational *necessity*.

It is written from the simple premise that the personal and the professional are not separate, and should not be separated out as if they were oil and water. The feelings of ambivalence that *afflict* this practitioner are never far from the surface as he works with organisations that contribute something to the ecologies of our existence.

This consultant recognises how convenient it is to keep the context of practice at arm's length. Economic demands can often shape a convenient reframe of the ethical reality. But it is the casual separation of conscious purpose from unconscious outcome that the writer has most in mind. When he talks about the "forces of fragmentation", he has in mind his own lived experience as a consumer, citizen, consultant and employee. He has in mind those moments where you are encouraged to drop your thinking down a level – to reduce, categorise, acquiesce – where imagination and multiplicity are just too inconvenient. This is when we stop noticing or caring any more, in the face of commercial pressures just to get the job done.

This, however, is more an account of what it could mean to have hope… where you feel you can make a difference in the world. Ambivalence should not be confused with inaction or apathy. Staying with it can bring accountability and a restlessness that shows up as passionate inquiry.

(Power, 2010b: 2)[1]

A Post-doctoral Metaphor

In the course of writing this chapter, I uncovered a new metaphor that, like curating, revealed an alternative way of understanding my intuitive approach and how I think about change more generally: the notion of a 'rhizome' (Deleuze and Guattari, 2004). I sometimes wonder where this would have taken me if I'd had it to hand during my doctoral inquiry. Now that I have come across it, it seems difficult to shake off.

Rhizome: in botany, horizontal, underground plant stem capable of producing the shoot and root systems of a new plant. This capability allows the parent plant to propagate vegetatively (asexually) and also enables a plant to perennate (survive an annual unfavourable season) underground. In some plants (e.g. water lilies, many ferns and forest herbs), the rhizome is the only stem of the plant. In such cases, only the leaves and flowers are readily visible.

Encyclopaedia Britannica

I like the idea that Ginger is categorised as a rhizome, as is crabgrass.

Both metaphors – the consultant as curator and the consulting process as rhizome – are woven through this chapter and have inspired its form. The curator in me wants to find a shape that is congruent with the content of this chapter and the rhizome metaphor encouraged me to avoid a standard 'beginning, middle and end' sequence. Thus stories from my practice are interspersed with reflections and with extracts from my doctorate, the result of a four-year inquiry process that greatly informed my thinking. This also gives you, the reader, the option to dip in and out, much as you can chose to wander around an exhibition as your interest takes you. You will notice a different typeface for different 'exhibits'.

Picasso's Head

I extract myself from the river of city commuters as we drain out of the underground system into the tributaries that lead to our respective office buildings. The innocuous doorway I step into belongs to the oldest institution of them all. Its

1   Image taken from *The Book of Urizen* by William Blake, 1794, British Museum, plate 17 (in Vaughan, 1999: 37).
"One Thought…" is taken from *The Marriage of Heaven & Hell* by William Blake, 1793, plate 8 (in Ostriker, 1977: 184).

Greco-Roman architecture is both *in* and *out* of place in this world. It goes back to an era that could be described as 'pre-modernity'. To many it is still a bastion of certainty in a troubled society. I would argue it has been seen (and conducts itself) as a 'tree' in all its steadfastness through the centuries. I wonder if it needs to be more *rhizome-like* in this 'post-modern' world.

I am here as a kind of process adviser and facilitator to an initiative that is concerned with uncovering those principles or values that lie at the heart of this newly merged institution. Part of the process involves a series of workshops with different hierarchical groupings. Both the previous organisations are represented equally in the room. The idea is to get an initial sense of what a hundred people (as a representative sample of 3,000) wish to uphold in their ways of working and how they would like their stakeholders to experience them. The longer-term aspiration is to develop a clearer sense of what this organisation stands for in 2013 and to enable employees to pay more conscious attention to these principles.

The approach I have advocated is based on storytelling and working with metaphor and visual imagery. Once this first phase has finished we will have 20 images and some words to stimulate a dialogue with the senior leaders. We are at the mid-point and already we have images of pillars, hands being joined, balanced scales, coats of arms and other representations of collaboration, integrity, solidity, rigour and public service.

Today one group created a line drawing, a recreation of a Picasso woman's head. It creates something of a stir. The group's explanation was along the lines of "we need somehow to look many ways and be on the leading edge of thinking... we need to be resilient, challenging and coherent. We represent familiarity and solidity and we have an eye to the future."

This is a traditional institution and reports have to be written. Peter (my client) will be writing a paper that captures the essence of the workshops, with a recommendation for the next phase. Our aim is to create a gallery of sorts so that the leadership team can immerse themselves in the imagery as they discuss the paper. From my research with professional curators, I learned that there is always one iconic image that speaks to the whole. This can appear at any stage of the curatorial process and becomes the focus for the brochures and posters that accompany the exhibition. It can often be experienced as a kind of 'catalyst' that generates multiple other ideas that are somehow imbued with the evocation of that one image. It is sometimes the 'game changer'.

I suggest to Peter we may have just found ours. I didn't realise until then that I was even looking for it. I now know I have been in *curator mode* from the beginning of this process.

Peter: They'll think we are losing the plot.

Kevin: But the image is already out there... it's been 'seen' by at least 20 people now. We didn't invent it. It's not *our* art work. And we have their words to go alongside it. Just think of the conversation it will provoke. This is not about being the essence of everything else but it conveys multiple meanings that we cannot control.

Peter: I'm not sure they will get it; we cannot just recreate this out of context.

Kevin: Well, whatever we think, it's now out there somewhere, *growing*.

[A few weeks later...]

I think Peter is right: we cannot do this out of context and we will need to think carefully about how we move on to the next phase of work. The spirit of Picasso's drawing has taken hold somehow – it keeps getting mentioned. We had always held onto the idea that the values work is an ongoing process of meaning making rather than a final outcome. It is not intended to be frozen in time but at some stage something will get written down that somehow captures the ethos of how people 'co-create' their working patterns and behaviours. The words might take root yet the very nature of change will mean new contexts and therefore multiple meanings over time.

unlike trees or their roots, the rhizome connects any point to any other point, and its traits are not necessarily linked to traits of the same nature; it brings into play very different regimes of signs, and even non-sign states. The rhizome is reducible neither to the One nor the multiple. It is not the One that becomes Two or even directly three, four, five, etc. It is not a multiple derived from the One, or to which One is added (n + 1). It is composed not of units but of dimensions, or rather directions in motion. It has neither beginning nor end, but always a middle (milieu) from which it grows and which it overspills.

(Deleuze and Guattari, 2004: 23)

THAT WAS THEN...

The Early Years

My MSc dissertation carried the title 'The Gentle Art of Reframing' as it was inspired by the work of Paul Watzlawick and his colleagues at the Mental Research Institute (MRI) in Palo Alto. As part of my inquiry, during late Spring in 2000, I had even flown out to California to meet him personally and join one of his workshops, called the 'The Therapy of As If'.[1] I spent the rest of my time hanging out in Monterrey with Professor Frank Barrett[2] and with an old work colleague in San Francisco. I was out on the West Coast for the best part of 10 days and spent

---

1   At the time, I was particularly interested in his therapeutic interventions in paradoxical situations and their potential application in an organisational context.
2   Frank was one of the co-authors behind the Appreciative Inquiry movement and nowadays is most associated with the use of jazz improvisational techniques as a metaphor for inspiring new ways of thinking about organisational behaviour and leadership. He is the author of *Yes to the Mess* (Barrett, 2012). He was particularly influential in my understanding of social constructionist ideas and had always encouraged me to continue with my academic studies to PhD level.

all of my free time visiting galleries, journaling, writing poetry and developing the core ideas that shaped my final paper. It's a well-worn cliché but I really did go on a journey for my dissertation research.

> During the heyday of the MRI, Gregory Bateson was out in Hawaii studying the behaviour of dolphins and developing his ideas about learning levels. He had gone back to his zoological roots and was expanding his interest *up a level* to communication patterns between organisms. His ideas anticipated the emerging field that is today known as bio semiotics. By the time it came to the early '70s, Bateson's work had sprouted up with a rhizome-like quality in the formal fields of studies that today we call biology, zoology, anthropology, cybernetics, sociology, psychology, learning and communications theory, ecology, urban design and aesthetics. *Steps to an Ecology of Mind* (Bateson, 2000) was his attempt to gather his ideas in one place.

I now wonder if I was over-invested in the idea that the Ashridge Masters in Organisation Consulting (AMOC) would be an end in itself. Maybe I was seduced by the possibility that finding a source of original wisdom would guide me over the following decades of my consulting career. However, the more I explored the work of the MRI and its history, the more I realised that I was opening up a wider and more complex web of ideas. It reached out beyond psychological and sociological frames to fundamental ontological questions about what it means to participate in the world. I couldn't ignore the fact that the pioneering family-therapy work of the MRI during the 1960s could be very clearly traced back to the ideas of Gregory Bateson, who had led a ground-breaking research project on communication patterns in family systems[1].

I had read everything that Watzlawick had written; was fascinated and inspired for a while and completed my dissertation. However, I realised that I was working at the surface, with a reduction of something far more profound. In the final few days of crafting my dissertation, I crafted a new introductory section of the paper to acknowledge the foundational influence of Bateson. Part of me felt like starting all over again but this was the best I could do at the time.

In the years that followed AMOC, I enjoyed reading more and more about Bateson and his life. I had a sense that I had stepped into the middle of a body

---

1   The MRI was established in 1959 by Don Jackson, John Weakland and Jay Haley who were all members of the Bateson project. The Bateson project was based down the road at Stanford University's VA Hospital in Palo Alto in the 1950s and became synonymous with pioneering ideas about human interactions and communications including double bind theory. The dominant paradigm for psychiatry then, as it often is today, was firmly focused on the dysfunctional behaviour of the individual. Bateson and his team drew a different boundary where the therapeutic focus was extended further to a 'web of interactions' that could include the family and even the therapist. In my world of consulting, this reinforced my own intuition that the interaction of relationships that we call an organisation is the 'patient', not any one individual or group of individuals. Behaviour is always in context.

of ideas that seemed to only make sense (to me) when taken together, not taken apart. Adrian McLean[1] and I ran the occasional workshop on Bateson and developed a burgeoning friendship fuelled by our passion for his work. In many ways I was already in research mode and this is where the yearning to do a doctorate began. I had to wait another six years. My aspiration was to pick up where I left off with my MSc studies and pursue my interest in Bateson's ideas. I had no desire to do this alone, with the occasional guidance of a PhD supervisor. The participative–relational and co-inquiring spirit of AMOC seemed to me to be the only congruent approach to this kind of research.

I finally took the idea of a doctorate to the AMOC faculty team in late 2004 and within 18 months a new doctoral-level programme had been launched.

A Blakean Inquiry

For many years now I have been fascinated by the art of William Blake. It was something about the compasses that first caught my curiosity. 'Newton'[2] and 'Ancient of Days'[3] typified his obsession with the forces of scientific reduction.

His work weaves a unique fabric of poems, prophesies and visual designs that connect with me on many levels. His artistic outpourings are the product of a person 'afflicted' by an unusual sensitivity to what is going on all around him. Yet these flights of imagination, though shrouded in symbols and imagery, were grounded in his here and now – a context that is a world (what he called 'Albion') in visible turmoil and transition. As I have become more familiar with his work, I have become more aware of a strong political and ethical dimension that sits in the shadows of his words and imagery. There were not many people in those times that were prepared to speak out in public about their concerns about what was happening in the name of progress. Religion, government and the monarchy were so deeply interdependent on each other that any voices of disapproval would be seen as a form of sedition or heresy. With this in mind, Blake chose to disguise his protest in the form of complex metaphor and symbolism; though he was rarely heard or understood, given that he had very little published in his lifetime. For me, his questions and concerns are still relevant to how we continue to construct (and destruct) our worlds into the twenty-first century, our here and now.

1 It would be remiss of me not to acknowledge the influence of Adrian, who was a member of the AMOC faculty and first introduced me to some of Watzlawick's and Bateson's ideas. He later became my dissertation supervisor.
2 'Newton' monotype by William Blake, 1795: Tate Britain (in Vaughan, 1999: 39)
3 'Ancient of Days' image of Urizen from *Europe: A Prophecy*, etched/painted by William Blake, 1793: British Museum (in Blindman, 2000: 174)

'Ancient of Days' by W. Blake

'Newton' by W. Blake

My take on wholeness, looking through the lens of Blakean mysticism, is an emerging sense of his reaction to a process of fragmentation that was going on during his lifetime. His 'Albion' was oppressed by religious dogma, scientific rationalism, relentless industrial incursions into the landscape. This was a society that to Blake was losing any sense of individuality or imagination... He feared that the soul of his beloved Albion was up for sale to the highest bidder. It is a familiar story.

(Power, 2010a: 109–10)

AMOC had challenged my deep-seated assumptions about the nature of change and how we construct reality. I discovered that words were not a pre-requisite for knowing and it now seems obvious that I would be drawn enthusiastically into the world of art and William Blake in particular. As is my pattern, I became fascinated by his life story and how that shaped his oeuvre as an engraver, poet and painter. Regular visits to the collections at the Fitzwilliam, Tate Britain and British Museum all deepened my interest and unintentionally became convenient research opportunities for my doctoral inquiry a few years later.

I remember Robin Ladkin's[1] advice in the first ADOC workshop: "Go back to the sources of a writer who has caught your attention, and then further to their sources and so on; this might even take you all the way back to Plato, in principle". With Gregory Bateson I didn't have to go too far. He acknowledged three enduring influences in his life: his father William, Samuel Butler the author and satirist, and William Blake!

I am not sure why I hadn't made this connection earlier. But there it was: an invitation to *hold together* two lines of inquiry that could not be held apart, to find a different way into Bateson's 'ecology of ideas' by engaging with Blake's work at a more profound level.

1   A member of the ADOC faculty who subsequently supervised my final thesis.

The 'Existential' Matters

Midway through ADOC, my research gaze necessarily returned to what this all might mean for my practice and why it could be of interest to other practitioners. There is no better impetus to learning than a consuming intellectual passion for a field of study. But on ADOC, this is not enough. It is fundamentally about *your* practice, not practice in a general, abstract sense, and ultimately it is about adding to knowledge to the field of practice. In that order.

My interest was to understand at a deeper level what I was prepared to stand for, which for me was no easy undertaking, given my *deeply* ambivalent nature. Existential and ethical concerns were all an inevitable part and what was going on in the rest of my life could not be somehow excluded for very long. To this day I vividly remember a moment during a client meeting in a local café, when my young son appeared with his nanny. He spotted me and became thoroughly upset when, after a brief hug, I had to return to my client. It was a particularly difficult and emotional time and the story of that encounter is recounted at some length in my thesis. It was a reminder that everything was becoming swept up in my inquiry, including my family life.

> What is happening right now is the shell that kept some sense of boundary, imperceptible as it is, between my worlds is starting to crack. Whatever identities I was clinging onto are crumbling away. I am a father first and foremost. Not a consultant. Not an aesthete. Not a pretender. Being a father is what perhaps needs to direct my impulses and intentions. Otherwise what exactly is it I am striving for?

(Power, 2010a: 44–7)

> *In every cry of every man,*
> *In every infant's cry of fear,*
> *In every voice, in every ban,*
> *The mind-forg'd manacles I hear*[1]

Why Curating?

> William Blake and Gregory Bateson were 'afflicted' with the ability to *see* more than we could ever imagine. They invited us to see patterns and ecologies of relationships through their unique contributions to worlds of art, science and ethics. My aesthetic engagement with their ideas has revealed a resonance with my own practice as a consultant who aspires to help others to see more of their own participation in the ecology of relationships of which they are part. I believe I am able to do this because I can *see* patterns of connection due to the nature of my inquiry method and the intuition that I have developed over many years. It has been suggested that my way of responding has a quality that is similar to the role of a curator.

(Power, 2010a: 134–5)

---

1   From 'London' in *Songs of Innocence and of Experience* by William Blake, 1794 (in Willmott, 1990: 38)

Part of the ADOC process requires participants to co-design and host their own learning experience. One particular workshop explored alternative ways of knowing through art and movement, in this case art works that we had all created spontaneously during a half day of free-form painting and collage work. We filled two rooms and a corridor with our efforts which were laid out in a gallery of sorts. The final part of our process was to tour our own gallery as a way of reflecting on themes and personal revelations from participating in the process. I shaped the layout of the 'exhibition' and adopted the role of facilitator and self-appointed tour guide.

Everybody has their own story of that day and I sensed something seemed to shift for each of our inquiries. For me, it was a throw-away remark by Bill Critchley[1] who proclaimed: "Kevin, you have just curated us".

I seem to have a highly developed sensitivity to the multiple perspectives that different people might bring to any given situation. Sometimes I see so many connections that I despair at the narrow set of factors that form the basis of a decision-making process. Indeed, I have realised that holding onto multiple truths rather than the one right way can actually be the best gift that I have to offer in my practice. I try to support others in discovering their own ambivalence, regardless of how uncomfortable it may get for them. It is hard work. Clients are looking for certainty and closure, being tentative and staying in inquiry mode is not easily valued.

A Curatorial Process?

An Elusive Definition

The nearest I can get to bringing more definition to this is to propose that there are five elements to a curatorial approach as a metaphor for my consulting practice:

1. A predisposition to reveal the perspectives that represent the organisation as a socially constructed phenomenon.

2. The act of making sense of these multiple perspectives as a participative process in a way that is insightful and provocative.

3. A determination to keep open layers of ambivalence rather than the natural inclination to reduce or synthesise.

4. It is about 'laying alongside' so that the patterns that connect can be revealed with a speculative zeal rather than premature analysis or definition

5. It is about keeping the bigger picture in mind... anything chosen has a Goethian quality in that whatever is exhibited says as much about the whole as it does about the part.

(Power, 2010a: 149–50)

---

1   Bill was a member of the ADOC faculty.

The incident at the ADOC workshop left me with the question: what actually does a curator do?

"…a practice that, in its constant changing among various possibilities, ultimately withdraws from any categorizing and escapes clear definition. It is an identity in perpetual transition, absorbing erratic social, geopolitical, ethnic, economic and other realities on a plateau of the intensely lived ordinary, and therefore resistant to the framing of a dictionary, guidebook or ready to use manual." (Maria Hlavajova in Kuoni, 2001: 81)

As an avid art enthusiast, I had always been fascinated with the curatorial choices made for an exhibition. Yet I had never paid attention to the process or assumptions that lay behind this particular role. This became the focus of the final phase of my research. It also influenced my decision to lay out my thesis as a series of metaphorical rooms in a gallery.

In the context of a gallery, the curatorial process requires the laying alongside of objects and artefacts as guided by a thematic flow or sequence. This could include: chronology, social history, methods and materials, peer influence, juxtapositions, political agendas, lifestyles, aesthetics and style, personal relationships, psychology and legacy which are all somehow represented in a coherent 'frame'. Identifiable boundaries and 'tidy delineations' are rare, although I would speculate that many contemporary curators would aim to subvert conventional norms around representation – preferring an originality and ethos that convey a particular concern or perspective. And of course space, accessibility and environmental concerns are all there to conspire against the realisation of any idealised concepts.

(Power, 2010a: 138)

The Strategy Day

Sue and I are setting up the room. The group we're working with are used to interacting by emails and telephone conferences and only occasionally in person. They have certainly never all been in a room together. And yet they have so much history with each other, many overlapping relationships and shared experiences over the years.

So here we are, moving sofas and easy chairs into the room and pinning posters onto the walls. Our intention is to create an environment conducive to working together in a different way. We want people to notice what it takes to have the conversations that matter. It is also a way for us, as consultants, to join the conversation, rather than be tempted into a performance. It is a place for us to make sense of whatever emerges between us.

I am reminded of Berthold Brecht's post-modernist concept of theatre, in which the separation between audience and actors collapses. The lights are left on and the actors approach exposes the whole idea of 'performance'; so that the audience are invited to reflect on their assumptions about the nature of theatre and how they participate in their experience.

We have had conversations with almost every person who represents this leadership group, 25 in total. They are in the middle of a reorganisation that is merging two areas of the business in order to create an integrated, less-fragmented experience for their clients and for themselves. Both realised that they couldn't exist without the other and yet had been unwittingly undermining each other constantly. Interestingly, most of these people have worked in both parts of the business and have crossed each other's paths at different stages in their careers, both inside and outside the organisation.

The reorganisation process has been initiated by three directors and, apart from a new structure and a high-level vision, almost everything else is still taking shape as the implications of the new world are emerging. Nobody is going to lose their jobs and yet feelings of exclusion, uncertainty, apathy and scepticism seem to be growing by the day. The more the directors have tried to communicate the changes, the less sense people are making of what it might all mean in reality. The very people who are being held responsible for making the changes happen cannot work out what this will mean for themselves, let alone for others.

My intuition is that this is a disparate group of individuals who need to 'see' each other as part of the same family. They need to get a sense of how they are all co-creating the conditions that trigger these feelings of uncertainty and anxiety. With hindsight it seems as if we are creating a metaphorical living room in which all of family life, functional and dysfunctional, can play out.

We haven't paid much attention to a load-bearing pillar, a thick metal pole, in the centre of the room. I enjoy finding creative ways of adapting to unusual spaces yet this unavoidable and immoveable object just seems to resist my imagination. For now it seems best to ignore or work around it somehow.

We start the first part of the workshop exploring the shared histories of everyone present. As part of this process we introduce the concept of 'dendrochronology' (tree-ring dating) as a metaphor for representing the collective story of the organisation. As participants organise themselves in 'tree rings', most people end up huddled around the pole in the centre of the room. It's as if the long-timers (who make up most of the group) are almost clinging to each other. The more recent joiners, with four to five years' (!) experience place themselves on the outside. We encourage each of the 'tree circles' to talk and share experiences which eventually leads to a whole-group conversation about their experience of the various "growth spurts and retrenchments" over the years.

All very insightful and yet I feel pressure building to move on to the next phase of the workshop agenda. Instead, as an experiment, I ask the group to reconfigure themselves to represent their current feelings of 'closeness' to what they now experience as the centre of the organisation. Without any hesitation, senior colleagues move out from the centre, even beyond some of their junior colleagues. The hierarchy seems to collapse, apart from the three directors who are predictably now hugging the pillar. Something palpable has happened and I decide to hold people here to reflect on how it feels to be standing in these new, sometimes distant, places in the room and to notice where their colleagues are. It may be uncomfortable but I also feel a sense of relief in the air. It's as if our agenda for the day has collapsed too. We are now talking about what is really going on for people.

This brings to mind some of the conversations that were part of my doctoral inquiry into the practice of curators in the arts world. As one of them said to me: "You either start with the full portfolio of work and then work out how the pieces will fit into the space. Or you start with the space in mind and notice what emerges from engaging with the artist's work, as a creative exchange." The latter approach seems most resonant with how I prefer to work.

Returning to My Roots

Aside from accounts of my practice, I chose to devote a separate 'gallery space' in my doctoral thesis to what I framed as the "roots of my practice". Curating is often imbued with a political dimension and it seemed inauthentic to ignore what lay behind some of my curatorial considerations.

In Room 2 there is a 'back-story' of someone who lived part of his childhood in a community that was once part of the inner-city landscape of 1960s Manchester. Home was a local corner shop in West Gorton where all of life passed through.

Image shown in Room 2: p. 67Image shown in Room 2: p. 68

It was a first experience of being a participant–observer in a social system where you neither felt *part of* nor felt *apart from*. It is as if this established a pattern of working in the 'in between' throughout various roles in organisations. This may explain in part how this consultant is able to take his particular stance.

But this is only part of the story, given that this thesis deals as much with the 'why' as with the 'how' of consulting. On further examination, the lost community of West Gorton was where this practitioner was first exposed to the effects of social engineering and the absence of voice for those affected. Social exclusion has its own connotations nowadays but this is about the implications of not knowing what you don't know through lack of aspiration and confidence. Hierarchy and privilege were never really questioned in those days because you assumed 'they up there' knew better.

The world of course has changed, yet the fuel for this inquiry (and indeed practice) seems to find its charge from an image of two boys on a street in Manchester. Or is it from the pathos of a photograph taken on the same street corner 40 or so years later?

This is a practitioner who treasures the idea and the possibility of 'community' because he knows what happens when communities no longer have a sense of possibility. He sees that in the workplace and he sees that in people's habitats and he sees that in nature. When he refers to the organisational and societal impact of fragmentation, he is also talking about the loss or the diminishment of 'voice'. It is no coincidence that this is the context for the work he finds himself drawn to.

(Power, 2010b: 3)

I left school at 16 and got the first job I could find in the midst of a recession that seemed to have the Northern British towns in its grip for longer than the rest of the country. Going to university seemed to me to be a perverse idea at the time. There is nothing unusual in any of that.

And yet I was becoming aware of things going on that were no longer acceptable to me as I entered adulthood. I was participating in a society that was losing touch with its soul, becoming anaesthetised and yet wide awake. I was a witness and therefore complicit in the corporate greed and ecological neglect that has defined the last few decades. It is too easy to blame 'them' out there, since we are also beneficiaries and contributors if we only stopped to look.

As a consultant–curator, I can actually do something other than just make a living and give clients what they demand. If I see my *life* as practice then perhaps this brings the extra responsibility to pay more attention to that which it is all too easy to turn a blind eye to, especially in our most vulnerable moments.

This inquiry is ultimately not a study of Bateson's or Blake's ideas. It is ultimately not a study of ambivalence or the metaphor of curating. It is an elusive pursuit of that which sometimes seems out of reach… it is about the possibility that I have the means to make a difference every so often. It is about finding the capacity to help others to find their own sparks of recognition of the patterns of relationships and how they are part of those patterns. This inquiry is about my struggle with and against our predisposition to want to separate out and reduce what we experience or want in the world into causal fragments. As organisational consultants, I think we have the capability to *disable* or *enable* the process of fragmentation, in either direction. And I despair that we often do not realise our direct *professional* contribution to a world that we profess to be concerned about.

(Power, 2010a: 211).

A Punctuation Point not an Ending

One of the conditions for my final thesis to be passed was for some kind of meta-commentary about what I had created – an overview that wouldn't become another room in the gallery. I agreed with the examiners that I would create an 'exhibition brochure' that would accompany the final publication. This became a six-page fold-out booklet that including some of the highlights of each room. The opening pages of this preview are shown at the beginning of this chapter. The front cover was a juxtaposition of a line of poetry from *The Marriage of Heaven and Hell* with an unrelated but highly evocative image, both from William Blake. For me it somehow evoked the intensity of my inquiry process and my relationship to my practice.

It was a final curatorial gesture and an attempt to bring a different kind of coherence to the whole affair. Like my master's experience, in the headiness of final completion, I realised this was just another step to formulating the next idea. It was another punctuation point but not an ending. If I were to repeat the process now, I *know* a different 'rhizome' would be emerging.

AND THIS IS NOW...

Already you will have noticed my deepening interest in *A Thousand Plateaus* (Deleuze and Guattari, 2004). My current attachment to their elusive ideas has a rhizome-like quality in itself and I realise I am only beginning to explore the possibilities of where this might take me. No doubt something else will 'pop up' further down the line but this is where I am right now.

> The rhizome operates by variation, expansion, conquest, capture, offshoots. Unlike the graphic arts, drawing or photography, unlike tracings, the rhizome pertains to a map that must be produced, constructed, a map that is always detachable, connectable, reversible, modifiable and has multiple entryways and exits and its own lines of flight. It is tracings that must be put on the map, not the opposite. In contrast to centred (even polycentric) systems with hierarchical modes of communication and pre-established paths, the rhizome is an acentred, non-hierarchical, non-signifying system without a General and without an organizing memory or central automaton, defined solely by a circulation of states.

> (Deleuze and Guattari, 2004: 23)

Rhizomatic thinking is essentially different from an arboreal model of thinking, where the tree with all its roots and connectedness below and above ground is the founding metaphor. A rhizome is different in that it has multiple root systems that can spring up anywhere. So it leads us to the idea of middles and in-betweens because there is no beginning or end.

Stepping into the Middle of a Conversation about Rhizomes[1]

JH: I want to know more about this rhizome metaphor as it seems to have really connected with you.

KP: Let me return to our first conversation. I said that owning up to my deep-seated ambivalence paradoxically has allowed me to become more committed. You immediately made a connection between

---

1   This chapter has *evolved out* from three separate conversations with John Higgins that took place in late 2012. This section is based on a particularly charged exchange of ideas after a sleepless night reading about rhizomes. I normally sleep well.

this paradox and identity, in particular the way in which people sometimes conflate their sense of self with their ideas. If the sense of who we are is too tightly bound up with our beliefs and ideas, then it can become immensely threatening when those ideas are challenged. Conversely, if I can hold my beliefs and ideas lightly, I can be less anxious about them and about whether they are right or wrong. To return to the rhizome metaphor: a tree stands and falls with its roots. A rhizome, on the other hand, with its network of roots, can much more easily survive when a large section of its root network is destroyed. In human terms, that would mean being less 'deeply rooted' and more open.

JH: I see a connection with Judi Marshall's notion of living life as inquiry and being able to pay more attention to the here and now, really seeing the moment.

KP: Yes, what Deleuze and Guattari are saying is that the 'middle' or 'held' state is by no means a state in which nothing happens. On the contrary, the middle is where things pick up speed. Similarly, they have structured their book in a way that allows you to dip in and out as you want. In fact, they positively encourage this instead of reading it in a linear, cover-to-cover way. This reminds me of the challenge I faced whenever I came up against the formal requirements of the academic system. It seemed to me to *demand* beginnings, middles and endings, in that order. I always wanted to start and finish in the middle when it came to my thesis. The only way I got myself out of this conundrum was by creating a gallery of sorts and by producing a curator's guide written as a third-person commentary.

JH: Can you say more about what you mean by 'the middle': its energy, its intensity?

KP: You can think of it as an expanding idea. As you engage with it, so ideas keep opening and then opening again.

JH: As you spoke I had the image of a flower bud bursting out and then the bud within the bud bursting and so on. It had the qualities of a Busby Berkeley musical number, something that's constantly unfolding.

KP: Like a kaleidoscope; yes, I'm drawn to that.

JH: Bateson talks about the importance of 'punctuation' in creating meaning. Was your doctorate a kind of Batesonian punctuation point? A point in your always-unfolding inquiry?

KP: Yes, but not in an upwards, downwards or linear sense. 'Recursive' seems like a good way to describe it. I like your notion of multiplicities within multiplicities. I have always been interested in the relationship between form and process, and in congruence between what we are talking about and how it is being represented or experienced. This is how I arrived at the concept for my final thesis and why it didn't make any sense to have a beginning, middle and end.

JH: I heard you mention something in the *Thousand Plateaus* book about 'the man'. I was struck by the conversation I had with Steve, where he also talked of 'the man'. If by this we mean the mindset of oppression or conformity, do you see yourself working for 'the man'?

KP: I realise that I'm railing against something which I'm also inevitably part of. I think that by accepting that I am part of it, in this wider circuit of connection, I'm able to stand apart from it. Only by seeing my participation am I able to work with it. I'm reminded of Blake's notion of "mind forg'd manacles".[1] It seems apt that he was talking about the mental repression of the poor people of London. Whereas I, for different reasons, am caught up in a different web that somehow constrains me from doing something meaningful. Meanwhile 'Rome' is metaphorically burning all around us.

It seems that small gestures of activism are all we have left and maybe that is what it will take. Can we reframe our relationship to what we are railing against? The least I can do as a consultant is to find ways of holding up whichever 'mirror' comes to hand and that means working with the light and the dark, the joy and the despair, the heaven and the hell. But of course, not everyone wants to go there.

JH: I'd like to stay with the experience of being part of what you despair of. I am involved in some evaluation work that felt dreadful at the outset – it seemed to have a very reductionist and punishing focus.

KP: Yes, I can relate to that. When I contract with clients, I do tell them sometimes that I am sceptical of what value is really created by any consulting intervention. That's different from separating myself from the situation and saying that a particular approach or issue is not my sort of thing. Here's my take on your experience of your evaluation work. Surely, it is not the act of evaluating that is the problem; it is *how* it gets done. A few years ago I'd have said "I want nothing to do with this; I have serious issues with evaluation." Now I'm trying to be less precious and work with whatever presents itself as a part of a potentially more generative 'whole'.

JH: A few years ago I'd have said I'm above all this! Now I'm more able to join people in their way of seeing things.

KP: Which reminds me of Charles Bukowski, the American writer. He was in many ways an outsider from society, a chronic alcoholic, a poet, a nihilist even, and he held down a job as a postman. He wrote about working for 'the man' in a really controlled and constraining environment. He found a way of writing dark, dark stuff... he was like a fetid Kerouac. You can almost smell him on the page, in the encounters he has and his relationships.

---

1   From 'London' in *Songs of Innocence and of Experience* by William Blake, 1794 (in Willmott, 1990: 38)

JH: Help me make the link with our conversation about how I am experiencing the evaluation work.

KP: We can all find ourselves doing the work that pays money. For Bukowski the value is not in the money per se, but in his other creative outputs that are stimulated by his extreme discomfort with his mundane, soulless, ritualised, demeaning existence. Similarly, the work I find myself despairing of can paradoxically be a source of real creativity, making me ask questions about why I find myself working here, how I am living my life and what I stand for. It can release a creative existential stream of thought that allows me to do more interesting work elsewhere. Some of the highest forms of art are stimulated by states of existential despair. The light and the dark are always in relationship. One doesn't exist without the other.

Curating an Ecology of Relationships

There is a moment in each day that Satan cannot find,
Nor can his Watch Fiends find it; but the Industrious find
This Moment & it multiply, & when it once is found
It renovates every Moment of the Day if rightly placed...

William Blake[1]

The importance of taking an ecological perspective reminds me of a consulting assignment I was involved in at a major city hospital. I was asked to facilitate a summit between a number of key people who were directly and indirectly impacting the performance of an Acute Assessment Unit, in which patients are kept under observation or awaiting a diagnosis following an emergency referral. It had become clear that pursuing waiting-time targets was not necessarily resulting in an improved patient experience through the system. Efforts to streamline bottlenecks in the process seemed to result in short-term improvements in one area by shifting the problem to another part of the hospital

As I accompany the clinical director around the emergency services area, I let my curiosity guide our wanderings and conversations. I stop to talk to different clinical and nursing staff, making dates for follow-up conversations or inviting them to the big day. Sometimes I am able to speak to patients in different stages of their treatment across the hospital. All the time I am playing with ideas for what we could do. I realise that my questions can seem random yet I am circling around different angles or perspectives to develop a richer picture than what has been presented. I am not as much looking for problems as for patterns that may or may not have some significance. It is about finding multiple perspectives that are perhaps known yet remain unarticulated *as a whole*.

This is my second day here and it is part of my immersion process. I am noticing recurring stories of what I can only describe as fragmentation and lack of cohesion. Yet I continue to be inspired by examples of amazing care within 'islands of excellence'. It is what happens in between these islands of care that impacts the

---

1   From 'Milton' by William Blake, 1804–1810 (in Blake, 1991: 172)

quality of the patient experience. That is what I am interested in, although I am conscious that it could be considered to be beyond the initial brief. I am revealing the web of relationships and connections that are not normally paid attention to because the level of complexity they present generates too much anxiety for already overloaded senior managers.

Before the summit, someone said that this cross section of people would never normally be seen in one place together. I noticed there were as many clinical uniforms as there were suits. That was symbolic somehow. These were people from all levels of seniority, upstream and downstream, who had come straight from the wards, the theatres and the offices. We even had GPs and others from the local primary- and social-care teams who had decided to show up. The room was packed as numbers had doubled from the original invitation list.

Mid-way through the morning I am asked to share my own insights as an 'outsider' (their words). The evening before, I had roughly sketched out two pictures: one showed the maps of relationships that had been described to me as part of my brief and the other showed how it now appeared to me following my immersion experience. The difference in complexity was remarkable. One of the clinical directors said to me afterwards: "Things started to shift for me after you showed that second picture. Everybody could see themselves in a much wider context and how everyone was contributing to the problem even though they were blaming others. What seemed to change the conversation was when one of the cardiologists said it looked just like an ecosystem and told his story about what happened after the rats were introduced onto an island. I think the penny dropped for us at that moment. There was no escaping the reality we were facing, which meant that we all had to change our behaviour."

…if I stay with the idea that my response is a curatorial one, the consultant has to complicate him- or herself to work with such complexity. This consultant therefore has to use that experience to guide the stakeholders through a sense-making process that is a curated experience of how the system in all its glory works and their role in it. But it cannot be broken down into its individual parts. It cannot be reduced into cause-and-effect dynamics. This is another example of Bateson's 'Mind' – cybernetic processes nested within cybernetic processes and within an environment of behavioural contexts – where, in my experience, only an aesthetic appreciation of these patterns that connect will have any chance of creating the necessary insight that leads to a different type of wisdom.

(Power, 2010b: 164–7)

Curating My Practice

Bateson developed his ideas about systems and ecological thinking through his grounding in the natural sciences and the arts; and through his sustained *rhizomatic* inquiries into bio-semiotic, anthropological and psychological phenomena. But these are my categorisations, not his. He did not see these delineations as they are all part of something inseparable. Something that we might want to call 'mind' or Gaia or whatever. I may not understand all of what Deleuze and Guattari have to say but I like the unbounded wildness and the experimentation of their work. I think their point is that *A Thousand Plateaus* is a 'rhizome' that is exploring the idea of a rhizome. It reverberates with a Blakean–Batesonian spirit of inquiry into the cultural, philosophical and political spheres of our human relating in the world.

Engaging with these kinds of inquiries inevitably draws me back to a 'meta' perspective, another level of abstraction. It involves theorising about theory, learning about what it takes to learn, developing a practice that is concerned about purpose and so on. It can lead to ambivalence and scepticism but it can also lead to a life-affirming curiosity about patterns of connection, paradoxical responses and revelatory juxtapositions.

A colleague once described my approach as tentatively revealing and disturbing the fixed patterns or assumptions held by a group or its members. He suggested that I would allow whatever needs to be said to unfold for as long as is needed, even when it might feel uncomfortable or unproductive to begin with. I think that's fine, as long as I also hold on to my responsibility and my contract with the group. I'd like to think that my approach is about *slowing down as a way of speeding up* the process.

It is as if I deliberately play into the role of the ringmaster, keeping a perspective on the emerging 'whole'. It certainly plays well to my ambivalence and yet I sometimes wonder what specifically the nature of my contribution is. Is it the act of convening, of designing, of ideation, of enabling sense-making and all the points in between? Is it about the idea of 'consulting practice' as a purpose-*full* idea? Maybe that's why I feel most useful as a change facilitator in situations where the content is to be negotiated between us, where I can come alongside what is emerging in relationship, rather than in a pre-set design.

I see my contribution as helping others (who are interested) to find some quality and purpose in what they do; to explore how they think and feel about their work as change agents and leaders. This means I have to pay attention to what I do and *don't do* as a practitioner.

Since I have finished my doctorate, I have become a core member of the faculty on an MSc and the programme director for a Postgraduate Certificate programme in Organisational Change. I am still very active with my organisational client work and am still fascinated by the implications of taking an ecological perspective in my practice. I am a husband, a son and a father of two young boys. Each role feeds the other and, more than ever, I see my life as becoming synonymous with a widening idea of practice. I used the idea of 'curating' in my thesis, perhaps because it is a helpful metaphor for how I engage with the multiplicities of my life and the stance that I hold onto in my work.

I am curating *us* and our context-laden ideas, not just *them*.

Bateson once said: "There is no such thing as a 'thing' in isolation". We are always in relation, in context, to the animate or inanimate other. And relationships are in constant flux or states of re-calibration. Towards the end of his life he wrote about the sacred and the imperative of our aesthetic engagement with the world. My refuge is my immersion in the arts in their many forms, in long walks in nature and in long winding conversations with friends. That is where I feel contained and where the world makes some sense, at least for a while.

This is where I will end, still in the middle of things, knowing that this rhizome will keep growing and finding new contexts and new forms. The work of the curator is never finished.

And so it has been in the final days of 'chipping away' where I am realising that any hints of dissatisfaction can never quite be extinguished. I feel like I am fumbling along… as I have tried to lay out my ecology of ideas to represent some kind of interconnected whole – something that reveals patterns of meaning that over time become "none of my business", as Seamus Heaney would say. It is elusive because I see any presentational form as inseparable from my inquiry. So if my art is an instinct to curate, perhaps my efforts to contain this 'untameable beast' – this *living inquiry* – can only be realised through a temporary construct that may work for today but then is always moving on and reforming itself. That is the central challenge that faces any curator as they try to make sense of something where meaning is in constant flux as time and context pass by.

(Power, 2010a: 207–8)

This Untameable Beast?[1]
The cistern contains,
The fountain overflows.

One thought fills immensity[2]

---

1   'The Great Red Dragon and the Woman Clothed with the Sun', watercolour by William Blake, circa 1806: ©Brooklyn Museum (in Vaughan, 1999: 53)
2   From *The Marriage of Heaven and Hell*, plate 8 by William Blake, 1793 (in Ostriker, 1977: 184)

CHAPTER 12

A Concluding Dialogue: Re-imagining the Practice of Change

In our final dialogue, we revisited our experience of working with the change doctors, the impressions we had of how their research continues to inform their practice and the sense we made of their stories. As we became increasingly energised in our sense-making process, the temptation to offer 'the' authoritative interpretation of their stories became almost irresistible, yet the irony of that aspiration was not lost on us. We have advocated rather vociferously that sense making is contextual, personal and fluid. At the same time the very project of writing a book betrays an aspiration to share our understanding with a wider audience, however fluid and contextual the nature of that understanding.

In that spirit we offer our thoughts as a punctuation in time, with the understanding that, by the time this book reaches you, our thinking will have evolved.

John: Across all the stories I see a puncturing of the old certainties of change management. The change doctors are pulling at the threads of what is taken as 'best practice', a rather tightly woven fabric in my view. They are challenging many of the basic assumptions that inform a programmatic, managed approach to change.

Kathleen: What, in your view, are the most significant of those assumptions?

John: A fundamental one, as I see it, is the notion that all change can be approached as if it is technical, rather than adaptive in nature. This results in large amounts of energy and resources being invested in planning and executing solutions that are unlikely to succeed, despite the fact that similar solutions failed on previous occasions. It's a typical example of an attempted solution becoming a problem in its own right; Watzlawick (1974) would call it "Trying harder".

Kathleen: It is strange, this human tendency to persist against all odds. Why do you think a mechanistic, rationalist approach to change is so pervasive? What makes the 'technical change illusion' so attractive?

John: To admit that we don't have answers is difficult at the best of times. Approaching a challenge as an adaptive one means admitting precisely that, to oneself and to those around us. That is a tall order, particularly for 'change experts'. Times of change provoke anxiety; anxious people want to be reassured. Leaders and consultants are expected to provide answers, not raise more questions. There is a connection with the notion of 'unsafe certainty', of course. It is really challenging to face up to the fact that there is no such position as 'safe certainty' in what Zygmunt Bauman called our "liquid times" or, less politely, in the words of a CEO client, "our bonkers pace of change".

Kathleen: Paradoxically, taking a technical approach to complex organisational challenges can compound the rate and pace of change that is inflicted on people, often quite unnecessarily but with devastating effect. One example is 'structure change'. It is a very popular intervention, maybe because rearranging the lines on an organisational chart appears tangible and straightforward. However, no amount of care in redrawing the reporting lines can really take into account the disruption that this causes in relationships. The scant attention for human needs is striking in our corporate world.

John: The change doctors challenge, each in their own way, the assumption that treating people as 'replaceable assets', rather than embodied, living and feeling people, is a sustainable proposition. It is ironic to consider how much of our 'defence against anxiety routines' involve denying our humanity, [the very thing] that caused us to feel anxious in the first place.

Kathleen: I experience that as a strong red thread across the different contributions: the challenge to our habitual instrumentalist approach to human engagement. This is subtle territory. For instance, the distinction between 'growth-in-connection' and developing people, including ourselves, solely with an ulterior purpose can be an elusive one, but it is discernible nonetheless. ADOC is a living example of that difference. As long as people participate with the sole purpose of getting a doctorate, their research fails to come alive. It is only when they are willing to engage fully with the process, and be changed by it in profound ways, that it reaches the depth of work that really makes a difference to our understanding of and engaging with organisations and change. Similarly trust that is in service of 'increased shareholder value', or similar abstract organisational objectives, is altogether of a different nature than the kind of 'proper' trust we associate with the private, home-and-friends sphere. The core distinction for me lies in the power dynamic underpinning our engagement. If we are willing to be changed by an encounter, to enter it from a position of mutuality, as Fletcher (1999) would call it, we honour our own humanity and that of the other.

In times of change and anxiety we need to feel connected, met at a profound level and held. There is no comfort or holding capacity in instrumental relationships. In my view, this is the most important work change agents can do: to truly meet and connect with people and support them in connecting with one another. Martin Buber (2004) called this an "I–Thou" relationship, in which we don't objectify the other but acknowledge our deep interdependence. He contrasts it with an objectifying, instrumentalising "I–It" approach, in which we treat the other as an object to be used. As a Jewish professor in Nazi Germany, Buber knew all about the catastrophic consequences of extreme commodification of human relating.

John: As you advocate the significance of mutuality, you have, perhaps inadvertently, got me started on a list... We have commented extensively on what we think is inappropriate and unhelpful in the way we go about changing organisations. I feel compelled to offer a set of alternatives, despite my advocacy of sense making being personal, social and contingent. I see a number of common characteristics in our change doctors and their work, which I believe are significant for all aspiring change agents.

Kathleen: Why not have a go at articulating them and offer them as food for thought?

John: OK. Presence would be first on my list. In my view, every one of the change doctors is wonderfully skilled at being present, wherever they turn up: in our inquiry meetings, with their clients in organisations, with their peers. They show up, fully, without becoming complicit in unhelpful patterns. They bring an embodied news of difference.

Kathleen: Although they are very different, bring their unique makeup, personal history and context, they all have a shared capacity for self-reflexivity in the moment. They have a wonderful ability to be present and be aware of their presence at the same time. They are all skilled at noticing themselves in their context in the midst of doing their work. The ability to fully participate and hold a sense of the whole, to keep perspective, is very powerful.

John: As I see it, this is what gives them the ability to create experiences of safe (enough) uncertainty. As they stand firmly in their ground, they can be fully present with what is unfolding, however challenging. They are not tempted to flee, or fight for that matter. They are past masters at side stepping the invitation to provide clients with the disabling illusion of safe certainty. Every one of them has invested intensively in their developing of their own roots and foundations. Their sustained inquiry into themselves and their practice has given them the confidence to tolerate, even welcome, the reality of not having the answers, whilst providing a safe enough container that allows others to engage constructively with doubt and unpredictability.

Kathleen: I think you are advocating the importance of first-person inquiry here? I would agree. The ability to act with awareness, to make informed choices and assess the effect of our actions in the moment is a core capability for any change agent. Much as we have made a distinction between instrumental trust and proper trust, or instrumental growth and 'growth-in-connection': I see a difference between self-awareness and quiet self-confidence on the one hand, and self-orientation and arrogance on the other. They are often confused and the diligent and sustained work that developing the former requires is all too readily dismissed as solipsistic, or self-obsessed, in organisations that have little time or patience for the discipline that this work requires.

John: I have been impressed with the discipline that the change doctors bring to all aspects of their work. Their ability to pay attention to a diversity and breadth of phenomena, whilst resisting the temptation to interpret or classify, is remarkable. They take experience seriously, their own and that of others. That means also paying attention to feelings and sensations as valuable sources of information. They invite others to notice what was overlooked, to pay close attention to their experience, right here, right now, rather than to rush off down the familiar and comforting paths of diagnosis, action and solution.

Kathleen: Staying with our experience, therefore, usually involves disrupting habitual patterns of acting and sense making. It is quite an art to be able to hold people in discomfort, inviting them to look again, from a different perspective. Looking for and surfacing patterns, rather than focussing on isolated symptoms, requires one to have the ability to be both fully present and keep attention for the whole. I see in every one of the change doctors, and in the practice that ADOC stands for, an exquisite ability to contain and provoke, all at once. If their practice was simply about containment then there would be no possibility for growth; if it was all about provocation, they would create such disturbance that they would trigger defensiveness, which is equally detrimental to learning and reflection. When they are at their best, they finely balance containment and provocation. It is what I aspire to and what I have seen you do in the process of writing this book.

John: For me, this way of understanding change and leadership is a rediscovery, or rather a recovery, of a craft. The type of change practices advocated by ADOC cannot be captured in a simple formula. Like any craft, it requires a careful honing of skills, a dedicated attention to the work in hand. It requires mastery and a deep insight into the nature of people and organisations, and in what it takes to bring difference in the world without turning the world against you.

Kathleen: This approach to change is both philosophical and practical. To quote Kurt Lewin, the father of Action Research: "There is nothing more practical than good theory"!

References

Anderson, L. (2006) Analytic Autoethnography. *Journal of Contemporary Ethnography*, 35(4), 373–95.

Anderson, R. (2006) Intuitive Inquiry: The Ways of the Heart in Research and Scholarship [Unpublished manuscript]. Retrieved 14 April 2009 from: http://www.wellknowingconsulting.org/publications/articles.html

Aposhyan, S. (2004) *Body–mind Psychotherapy: Principles, Techniques and Practical Applications*. New York, NY: W. W. Norton.

Bahnisch, M. (2000) Embodied Work, Divided Labour: Subjectivity and the Scientific Management of the Body in Frederick W. Taylor's 1907 'Lecture on management'. *Body and Society*, 6(2), 51–68.

Baier, A. (1994) *Moral Prejudices*. Cambridge, MA: Harvard University Press.

Bainbridge Cohen, B. (1994) *Sensing Feeling and Action: The Experiential Anatomy of Body–mind Centering*. Northampton, MA: Contact Editions.

Bakan, D. (1996) *The Duality of Human Existence*. Chicago, IL: Rand McNally.

Barrett, F.J. (2012) *Yes to the Mess: Surprising Leadership Lessons from Jazz*. Boston, MA: Harvard Business Review Press.

Barry, D., and Hazen, M. (1996) Do You Take Your Body to Work? In D. Boje, R. Gephart and T. Thatchenkery (eds), *Postmodern Management and Organization Theory*. Thousand Oaks, CA: Sage.

Bateson, G. (1958) *Naven: A Survey of the Problems Suggested by a Composite Picture of the Culture of a New Guinea Tribe Drawn from Three Points of View* (2nd ed.). Stanford, CA: Stanford University Press.

Bateson, G. (2000) *Steps to an Ecology of Mind*. Chicago, IL: University of Chicago Press.

Bateson, G. (2002) *Mind and Nature: A Necessary Unity*. New York, NY: Hampton Press.

Bateson, G., and Bateson, M.C. (1987) *Angels Fear: Investigation into the Nature and Meaning of the Sacred*. New York, NY: Macmillan.

Belenky, M., Clinchy, B., Goldberger, N., and Tarule, J. (1997) *Women's Ways of Knowing: The Development of Self, Voice and Mind* (10th ed.). New York, NY: Basic Books.

Berger, J. (1972) *Ways of Seeing*. London: BBC/Penguin.

Bidault, F., and Castello, A. (2010) Why too much trust is death to innovation. *MIT Sloan Management Review*, 51(4), 33–8.

Biggs, D., Matthewman, L., and Fultz, C. (2012) Romantic relationships in organisational settings: Attitudes on workplace romance in the UK and USA. *Gender in Management: An International Journal*, 27(4), 271–85.

Bindman, D. (ed.) (2000) *William Blake: The Complete Illuminated Books*. London: Thames & Hudson.

Blake, W. (1804–1820/1951) Jerusalem: The Emanation of the Giant Albion, Chapter 3 [illustration], (Plate 55). London: Trianon Press.

Blake, W. (1991) *Poems and Prophecies*. London: Everyman's Library.

Bortoft, H. (1996) *The Wholeness of Nature: Goethe's Way of Science*. Edinburgh: Floris Books.

Brady, I. (2008) Poetics for a Planet. In N.K. Denzin and Y.S. Lincoln (eds), *Collecting and Interpreting Qualitative Materials* (pp. 501–64). Thousand Oaks, CA: Sage.

Brook, P. (1996) *The Empty Space*. New York, NY: Touchstone.

Bruhn, J.G. (2001) *Trust and the Health of Organizations*. New York, NY: Kluwer.

Buber, M. (2004) *I and Thou*. London: Continuum.

Bukowski, C. (1992) *Post Office*. London: Virgin Books.

Burr, V. (2003) *Social Constructionism*. New York, NY: Routledge.

Campbell, J. (1949) *The Hero with a Thousand Faces*. Princeton, NJ: Princeton University Press.

Campbell, J. (1999) *The Hero's Journey: Joseph Campbell on his Life and Work*. Boston, MA: Element Books.

Casement, P. (2002) *Learning from our Mistakes: Beyond Dogma in Psychoanalysis and Psychotherapy: Psychoanalysis and Beyond*. London: Routledge.

Chase, S. (2008) Narrative Inquiry. In N.K. Denzin and Y.S. Lincoln (eds), *Collecting and Interpreting Qualitative Materials* (pp. 57–94). Thousand Oaks, CA: Sage.

Covey, S.M.R. (2006) *The Speed of Trust: The One Thing that Changes Everything*. New York, NY: Simon and Schuster.

Cunliffe, A. (2009) *A Very Short, Fairly Interesting and Reasonably Cheap Book about Management*. Los Angeles, CA: Sage.

Day, A., and Power, K. (2009) Developing Leaders for a World of Uncertainty, Complexity and Ambiguity. *360°, the Ashridge Journal*, (Winter), 20–25.

Deleuze, G., and Guattari, F. (1980/2004) *A Thousand Plateaus: Capitalism and Schizophrenia*. London: Continuum.

Denzin, N.K., and Lincoln, Y.S. (eds) (2008) *Collecting and Interpreting Qualitative Materials*. Thousand Oaks, CA: Sage.

Edinger, E.F. (1985) *Anatomy of the Psyche: Alchemical Symbolism in Psychotherapy*. Chicago, IL: Open Court.

Elias, N. (1994) *The Civilizing Process: Sociogenetic and Psychogenetic Investigations,revised edition* (2000) (E. Jephcott, Translation.). Oxford: Blackwell Publishing.

Ellis, C. (1999) Heartfelt Autoethnography. *Qualitative Health Research*, 9(5), 669–83.

Ellis, C., and Bochner, A.P. (eds) (1996) *Composing Ethnography: Alternative Forms of Qualitative Writing*. Walnut Creek, CA: AltaMira Press.

Erdman, D.V. (ed.) (1965) *The Complete Poetry and Prose of William Blake*. New York, NY: Doubleday.

Fineman, S. (ed.) (2000) *Emotion in Organizations*. London: Sage.

Fisher, D., and Torbert, W.R. (1995) *Personal and Organizational Transformations: The True Challenge of Continual Quality Improvement*. London: McGraw-Hill.

Fletcher, J.K. (1999) *Disappearing Acts. Gender, Power, and Relational Practice at Work*. Cambridge, MA: MIT Press.

Fontana, A., and Frey, J. (2008) The Interview: From the Neutral Stance to Political Involvement. In N.K. Denzin and Y.S. Lincoln (eds), *Collecting and Interpreting Qualitative Materials* (pp. 115–60). Thousand Oaks, CA: Sage.

Freeman, J. (2010) *Blood, Sweat and Theory: Research through Practice Performance*. London: Libri.

Gergen, K.J. (1999) *An Invitation to Social Construction*. London: Sage.

Goleman, D. (1996) *Emotional Intelligence: Why it Can Matter More than IQ*. London: Bloomsbury.

Grosz, E.A. (1994) *Volatile Bodies: Toward a Corporeal Feminism*. Bloomington, IN: Indiana University Press.

Harding, N. (2002) On the Manager's Body as an Aesthetic of Control. *TAMARA: Journal of Critical Postmodern Organization Science*, 2(1), 63–76.

Hartley, L. (ed.) (2009) *Contemporary Body of Psychotherapy: The Chiron Approach*. Hove: Routledge.

Heifetz, R.A. (1994) *Leadership without Easy Answers*. Cambridge, MA: Harvard University Press.

Heron, J. (1992) *Feeling and Personhood: Psychology in Another Key*. London: Sage.

Heron, J. (1996) *Co-operative Inquiry: Research into the Human Condition*. London: Sage.

Hughes, J. (2006–2009) *Personal Journal*. Unpublished manuscript.

Hughes, J. (2010) *An Inquiry into Trust: Confronting My Practice as an Organisational Consultant* (Unpublished Doctoral thesis). Berkhamsted: Ashridge/Middlesex University.

Hunt, C. (2009) They pass by themselves without wondering: Using the self in, and as, research. In *Really Useful Research: Critical Perspectives on Evidence-Based Policy and*

Practice in Lifelong Learning: Proceedings of the 39th Annual SCUTREA Conference (pp. 255–62). University of Cambridge.

Jordan, J.V., Kaplan, A.G., Baker Miller, J., Stiver, I.P., and Surrey, J.L. (1991) *Women's Growth in Connection: Writings from the Stone Center*. New York, NY: The Guilford Press.

Jung, C.G. *The Collected Works, trans. RFC Hull,* ed. H.Read, M.Fordham, G.Adler, W.McGuire. London: Routledge and Kegan Paul.

(1953) Volume 12, *Psychology and Alchemy.*

(1954) Volume 16, *The Practice of Psychotherapy: essays on the psychology of the transference and other subjects.*

(1959) Volume 9, part II *Aion: researches into the phenomenology of the self.*

(1967) Volume 13, *Alchemical Studies.*

Jung, C.G. (1958) *The Undiscovered Self*. New York, NY: Signet.

Jung, C.G. (1983) *Memories, Dreams and Reflections*. London: Fontana Press.

Kemmis, S., and McTaggart, R. (2000) Participatory Action Research. In N.K. Denzin and Y.S. Lincoln (eds), *Handbook of Qualitative Research* (2nd ed., pp. 567–606). Thousand Oaks, CA: Sage.

King James Bible (1839) London: Collins and Company.

Koenings, M., and Tranel, D. (2007) Irrational Economic Decision-making after Ventromedial Prefontal Damage: Evidence from the Ultimate Game. *The Journal of Neuroscience*, 27(4), 951–6.

Kuoni, C. (ed.) (2001) *Words of Wisdom: A Curator's Vade Mecum on Contemporary Art*. New York, NY: Independent Curators International.

Lakoff, G., and Johnson, M. (1999) *Philosophy of the Flesh: The Embodied Mind and its Challenge to Western Thought*. New York, NY: Basic Books.

Lather, P. (1991) *Getting Smart: Feminist Research and Pedagogy with/in the Postmodern*. New York, NY: Routledge.

Lather, P. (1993) Fertile Obsession: Validity after Poststructuralism. *The Sociological Quarterly*, 34(4), 673–693.

Linstead, H., and Hopfl, H. (eds) (2000) *The Aesthetics of Organization*. London: Sage.

Lipset, D. (1980) *Gregory Bateson: The Legacy of a Scientist*. Englewood Cliffs, NJ: Prentice Hall.

Maister, D.H., Green, C.H., and Galford, R.M. (2002) *The Trusted Advisor*. New York, NY: Simon & Schuster.

Marsh, S. (2009) *The Feminine in Management Consulting*. London: Palgrave Macmillan.

Marshall, J. (1999) Living Life as Inquiry. *Systemic Practice and Action Research*, 12(2), 155–71.

Marshall, J. (2001) Self-reflective Inquiry Practices. In P. Reason and H. Bradbury (eds), *Handbook of Action Research: Participative Inquiry and Practice* (pp. 433–9). London: Sage.

Marshall, J., and Reason, P. (2008) Taking an Attitude of Inquiry. In B. Boog, J. Preece, M. Slagter and J. Zeelen (eds), *Towards Quality Improvement of Action Research: Developing Ethics and Standards* (pp. 61–81). Rotterdam: Sense Publishers.

Mason, B. (1993) Towards Positions of Safe Uncertainty. *Human Systems: The Journal of Consultation & Management* 4, 189–200.

McDonald, P. (2012) Workplace Sexual Harassment 30 Years on: A Review of the Literature. *International Journal of Management Reviews*, 14(1), 1–17.

McGuire, J., Palus, C., and Torbert, B. (2008) Toward Interdependent Organizing and Researching. In A. Shani, S. Mohrman, W.A. Pasmore, B. Stymne and N. Adler (eds), *Handbook of Collaborative Management Research* (pp. 123–42). Thousand Oaks, CA: Sage.

McIlveen, P. (2008) Autoethnography as a Method for Reflexive Research and Practice in Vocational Psychology. *Australian Journal of Career Development*, 17(2), 13–20.

McNiff, J., and Whitehead, J. (2006) *All You Need to Know about Action Research*. London: Sage.

Menzies, I.E.P. (1960) Social Systems as a Defence against Anxiety: An Empirical Study of the Nursing Service of a General Hospital. In E. Trist and H. Murray (eds), *The Social Engagement of Social Science, Volume 1: The Socio-psychological Perspective*. London: Free Association Books.

Miller, J.B. (1986) *Toward a New Psychology of Women*. Boston, MA: Beacon Press.

O'Driscoll, D. (2008, 8 January) Interview with Seamus Heaney. *Guardian*, p. 2.

Olesen, V. (2000) Feminisms and Qualitative Research at and into the Millenium. In N.K. Denzin and Y.S. Lincoln (eds), *Handbook of Qualitative Research* (2nd ed., pp. 215–56). Thousand Oaks, CA: Sage.

Ostriker, A. (ed.) (1977) *William Blake: The Complete Poems*. Harmondsworth: Penguin.

Pasmore, W.A., Stymne, B., Shani, A.B., Mohrman, S.A., and Adler, N. (2008) The Promise of Collaborative Management Research. In A.B. Shani, S.A. Mohrman, W.A. Pasmore, B. Stymne and N. Adler (eds), *Handbook of Collaborative Management Research* (pp. 7–32). Thousand Oaks, CA: Sage.

Pfeffer, J., and Sutton, R.I. (2006) *Hard Facts, Dangerous Half-truths, and Total Nonsense: Profiting from Evidence-based Management*. Boston, MA: Harvard Business School.

Pfister, H.R., and Böhm, G. (2008) The Multiplicity of Emotions: A Framework of Emotional Functions in Decision Making. *Judgement and Decision Making*, 3(1), 5–17.

Plunkett, M. (2001) Serendipity and Agency in Narrative of Transition: Young Adult Women and their Careers. In D. McAdams, R. Josselson and A. Lieblich (eds), *Turns in the Road: Narrative Studies of Lives in Transition* (pp. 151–76). Washington, DC: American Psychological Association.

Polanyi, M. (1958) *Personal Knowledge: Towards a Post-critical Philosophy*. London: Routledge and Kegan Paul.

Polkinghorne, D. (2007) Validity Issues in Narrative Research. *Qualitative Inquiry*, 13(4), 471–86.

Power, K. (2010a) 'The Consultant as Curator: A Blakean Inquiry into Practice as Vocation', (Unpublished Doctoral thesis). Berkhamsted: Ashridge/Middlesex University.

Power, K. (2010b) *One Thought Fills Immensity: Curator's Guide to 'The Consultant as Curator'* (Unpublished Doctoral thesis). Berkhamsted: Ashridge/Middlesex University.

Pretat, J. (1994) *Coming to Age: The Croning Years and Late-life Transformation*. Toronto, ON: Inner City Books.

Pullman, P. (1997) *The Subtle Knife*. London: Scholastic Children's Books.

Raine, K. (2002) *Blake and Antiquity*. London: Routledge.

Read, H. (ed.) (1966) *The Collected Works of C.G. Jung, Volume 16: The Practice of Psychotherapy: Essays on the Psychology of the Transference and Other Subjects*. (R.F.C. Hull, Trans.) (2nd ed.). New York, NY: Pantheon Books.

Read, H. (ed.) (1967) *The Collected Works of C.G. Jung, Volume 13: Alchemical Studies* (R.F.C. Hull, Trans.). Princeton, NJ: Princeton University Press.

Read, H. (ed.) (1981) *The Collected Works of C.G. Jung, Volume 9, Part 1: The Archetypes and the Collective Unconscious* (R.F.C. Hull, Trans.) (2nd ed.). Princeton, NJ: Princeton University Press.

Read, H., and Fordham, M. (eds) (1980) *The Collected Works of C.G. Jung, Volume 12: Psychology and Alchemy* (R.F.C. Hull and G. Adler, Trans.) (2nd ed.). Princeton, NJ: Princeton University Press.

Reason, P. (1997, August) *Revisioning Inquiry for Action: A Participatory Review*. Invited Address at the Academy of Management Annual Conference. Boston, MA

Reason, P., and Bradbury, H. (2001) Introduction: Inquiry and Participation Research in Search of a World Worthy of Human Aspiration. In P. Reason and H. Bradbury (eds), *Handbook of Action Research: Participative Inquiry and Practice* (pp. 1–14). London: Sage.

Reason, P., and Marshall, J. (1987) Research as Personal Process. In D. Boud and V. Griffin (eds), *Appreciating Adults Learning: From the Learner's Perspective* (pp. 112–26). London: Kogan Page.

Reason, P., and Torbert, W. (2001) The Action Turn: Toward a Transformational Action Science. *Concepts and Transformation*, 6(1), 36–52.

Reynolds, L. (1997) *The Trust Effect: Creating the High Trust, High Performance Organization*. London: Nicholas Brealey.

Richardson, L. (1994) Writing: A Method Inquiry. In N.K. Denzin and Y.S. Lincoln (eds), *Handbook of Qualitative Research* (pp. 516–29). London: Sage.

Richardson, L., and St. Pierre, E.A. (2008) Writing: A Method of Inquiry. In N.K. Denzin and Y.S. Lincoln (eds), *Collecting and Interpreting Qualitative Materials* (pp. 345–71). London: Sage.

Rogers, C. (2004) *On Becoming a Person: A Therapist's View of Psychotherapy*. London: Constable & Robinson.

Rose, G. (2012) *Visual Methodologies* (3rd ed.). London: Sage.

Rosenwald, G.C., and Ochberg, R.L. (1992) *Storied Lives: The Cultural Politics of Self-understanding*. New Haven, CT.: Yale University Press.

Rugg, J., and Sedgwick, M. (eds) (2007) *Issues in Curating Contemporary Art and Performance*. Bristol: Intellect Books.

Scharmer, C.O. (2008) *Theory U: Leading from the Future as it Emerges*. San Francisco, CA: Berrett-Koehler.

Seeley, C. (2011, June) *A Thought Piece on Artful Knowing for a Sustainable Future*. Paper Presented at the Ashridge International Research Conference, Berkhamsted.

Sennett, R. (2006) *The Culture of the New Capitalism*. New Haven, CT: Yale University Press.

Sewall, L. (1999) *Sight and Sensibility: The Ecopsychology of Perception*. New York, NY: J.P. Tarcher/Putnam.

Shaw, P. (2001) *Changing Conversations in Organizations*. London, Routledge.

Shotter, J. (1993) *Cultural Politics of Everyday Life: Social Construction and Knowing of the Third Kind*. Buckingham: Open University Press.

Simon, H. (1989) Making Management Decisions: The Role of Intuition and Emotion. In W.H. Agor (ed.), *Intuition in Organizations: Leading and Managing Productively* (pp. 23–39). Newbury Park, CA: Sage.

Staunton, T. (ed.) (2002) *Body Psychotherapy*. London: Brunner-Routledge.

Tannahill, R. (1988) *Food in History* (2nd rev. ed.). London: Penguin.

Taylor, F.W. (2008) Report of a Lecture by and Questions put to Mr F.W. Taylor: A Transcript. *Journal of Management History*, 14(3), 214–36.

Taylor, S.S., and Hansen, H. (2005) Finding Form: Looking at the Field of Organizational Aesthetics. *Journal of Management Studies*, 42(6), 1,211–31.

Torbert, W.R. (1991) *The Power of Balance: Transforming Self, Society and Scientific Inquiry*. London: Sage.

Torbert, W.R. (2001) The Practice of Action Inquiry. In P. Reason and H. Bradbury (eds), *Handbook of Action Research: Participative Inquiry and Practice* (pp. 250–60). London: Sage.

Torbert, W.R. (2004) *Action Inquiry: The Secret of Timely and Transforming Leadership*. San Francisco, CA: Berrett-Koehler.

Totton, N. (2002) Foreign Bodies: Recovering the History of Body Psychotherapy. In T. Staunton (ed.), *Body Psychotherapy* (pp. 7–26). Hove: Brunner-Routledge.

Trethewey, A. (1999) Disciplined Bodies: Women's Embodied Identities at Work. *Organization Studies*, 20(3), 423–50.

Vaughan, W. (1999) *William Blake*. London: Tate Publishing.

Wadsworth, Y. (2008) Action Research for Living Human Systems. In B. Boog, J. Preece, M. Slagter and J. Zeelen (eds), *Towards Quality Improvement of Action Research* (pp. 45–60). Rotterdam: Sense Publishers.

Watzlawick, P. (1974) *Change: Principles of Problem Formation and Problem Resolution*. New York, NY: W.W. Norton.

Watzlawick, P. (1990) *Munchausen's Pigtail: Or Psychotherapy and Reality*. New York, NY: W.W. Norton.

Watzlawick, P., Bavelas, J.B., and Jackson, D. (1967) *Pragmatics of Human Communication: A Study of Interactional Patterns, Pathologies and Paradoxes*. New York: W.W. Norton & Co.

Weisbord, M. (2012) Productive Workplaces: Dignity, Meaning and Community in the 21st Century. San Francisco, CA: Jossey-Bass.

Wilber, K. (1996) *A Brief History of Everything*. Boston: Shambhala Publications.

Willmott, R. (ed.) (1990) *Songs of Innocence and of Experience*. Oxford: Oxford University Press.

Wollstonecraft, M. (2004) *A Vindication of the Rights of Women* (rev. ed.). London: Penguin Classics.

Young, E. (2012) Alimentary Thinking. *New Scientist*, 216(2,895), 38–42.